KT-406-009

THE HORSE AND THE LAW

Also by Donald Cassell
The Photographer and the Law

THE HORSE
AND THE LAW

Donald Cassell

Consultant Editor
Richard Gordon, MA, Ll.M.,
Barrister-at-Law

DAVID & CHARLES
Newton Abbot   London   North Pomfret (Vt)

While the author and publishers have taken every care in the production of this book, they can accept no legal responsibility for any errors which may have occurred.

British Library Cataloguing in Publication Data

Cassell, Donald
 The horse and the law.
 1. Horses — Law and legislation —
 England
 I. Title
 344.2064'7   KD667.H6

 ISBN 0-7153-8813-4

© Donald Cassell 1987

All rights reserved. No part of this
publication may be reproduced, stored
in a retrieval system, or transmitted,
in any form or by any means, electronic,
mechanical, photocopying, recording or
otherwise, without the prior permission
of David & Charles Publishers plc

Photoset in Plantin by
Northern Phototypesetting Co, Bolton
and printed in Great Britain
by A. Wheaton & Co Ltd, Hennock Road, Exeter
for David & Charles Publishers plc
Brunel House, Newton Abbot, Devon

Published in the United States of America
by David & Charles Inc
North Pomfret, Vermont 05053, USA

Contents

Contents

Introduction

According to Shakespeare, Richard III at Bosworth Field would have given his kingdom for a horse – hyperbolic, perhaps, but some indication of the value which has been placed on horses for centuries. In fact the horse has played a prominent role in the history of mankind since the animal was first domesticated which, experts believe, was some time prior to 2000BC.

In war, the horse has been used to draw chariots and later field guns, to say nothing of its role in the countless cavalry charges which have altered the course of many a battle. In peace, it has been used for transportation and agricultural purposes and has opened up hitherto unexplored areas of the globe.

It was because of the importance that man placed on the horse for all these uses, and many more, that it was prized and protected far more than the average man or woman. In the old days people were hanged for stealing a horse and many Acts of Parliament concerning the horse passed in the nineteenth century remain in force.

Today the horse is used mainly for pleasure. Not many years ago ownership of a horse was very much the prerogative of either the farmer or the wealthy. Although still comparatively expensive animals to buy and to keep, horses are owned by more and more people from all walks of life, either outright or in partnership, while many more enthusiasts hire an animal for weekly riding sessions. As a result the average man, woman and child who has anything to do with horses or ponies may find themselves more likely to be involved with the criminal and civil law than they might otherwise have been.

The criminal and civil law can affect both the way the horse is ridden and its ownership, and other matters affecting its use. Criminal law forms a very small body of Parliamentary legislation and what is known as common law. It can best be described as that part of the law which either Parliament or custom, over many years, has declared to be antisocial, breach of which results in the imposition on the offender of penal sanctions such as fines or imprisonment. The civil law can be said to serve a dual purpose: first, to provide a framework within which we conduct our everyday business and, second, to provide a remedy for any wrong which others may do to us.

It is within this framework that there has grown up over the past twenty-five years or so what has become known as consumer law. This affects our everyday life as customer, tradesman or supplier of services and this section of the law will figure prominently in the following pages. It is worth remembering that unless the rights of consumers are enforced, they will wither and die.

Readers will notice that when the civil law is discussed, there are many references to the reasonable man and reasonable standards of behaviour. In civil law what is or is not reasonable is so often the yardstick by which cases are judged.

1 FIRST, GET YOUR HORSE

A horse is sold as 'free from vice'
but within days it displays bad habits.

Does the buyer have a legal remedy?

It is arguable that there is nothing more calculated to cause tears, bitterness, frustrations and, in some cases, financial loss, than buying a horse without taking the elementary precaution of having the animal examined by a veterinary surgeon or, if something has gone wrong for which the law provides a remedy, being unable to enforce a legal right through ignorance of its existence.

At one time it was very much the case of *caveat emptor* – let the buyer beware – when it came to buying a horse but today the Sale of Goods Act 1979 provides protection for buyers who purchase a horse or pony from a dealer. This Act, which superseded a remarkably similar one of the same title passed in 1893 on which much case law is still based, plays an important part in that corpus of consumer law which has proliferated in the last two or three decades. The Act does not afford protection where *private* sales are concerned – though there are other safeguards – unless the seller is, in fact, a dealer holding himself out to be a private seller.

The remedy for a dissatisfied purchaser (as a result of a private sale) lies in suing for breach of contract. The sale and purchase of a horse or pony is a contract, whether the agreement be in writing or made verbally, and contract will be the basis of much which is discussed in this and later chapters.

A contract is an agreement whereby a person agrees to sell goods or services in return for valuable consideration which may be either money – which is the usual case – or some other form of recompense, always provided that it is not illegal, against public policy or morals. To the layman the term 'valuable consideration' may be misleading: it does not mean, for instance, that a horse worth £5,000 has to be sold for that amount for the contract to be valid. Provided both sides are in agreement and there is no question of fraud or duress, if the horse in the above example was sold for £5 or even 5p this would be rated as valuable consideration.

For ease of narrative and to avoid confusion in the mind of the reader, the remainder of this chapter will deal with the purchase of a horse as a result of a private sale, to which the protection and conditions of the Sale of Goods Act do not apply, as well as buying a horse in partnership, leasing and importing a horse.

Obtaining a warranty

All potential buyers of a horse or pony from a private seller are advised to obtain an express warranty on such important points as age, fitness for, say, hunting or whatever purpose it is required, as well as a general warranty that the animal is free from vice. In this respect 'vice' in a horse has a precise meaning: it covers one or more bad habits such as wind sucking, kicking, bolting, or biting.

It is also common sense for a purchaser to get a warranty to cover the soundness of the horse but such a warranty would not cover defects that would be patently obvious by inspection of the animal. A horse is unsound in the legal sense if, at the time of sale, it has any disease which lessens, or during the progress of the ailment will lessen, the natural usefulness of the animal. But it is no use a buyer relying on this unless he has received a warranty of soundness from the seller.

One cannot assume that all those with a horse to sell are honourable: many are but, unfortunately, there are some who are not. The latter can be likened to the mythical second-hand car salesman who has only a nodding acquaintance with truth and accuracy when it comes to selling a car. So it cannot be stressed with sufficient force how important it is for the buyer to receive some documentation which includes a warranty as to fitness and freedom from vice. No reputable seller should cavil at giving such a warranty.

This leads to the importance of having a proper contract of sale. (A specimen contract is shown on page 26.)

Buying on approval

From time to time horses are sold on approval and unless both parties to the transaction have a clear understanding of what is involved, there is a potential source of conflict and eventual litigation. Although a verbal agreement or contract is just as binding as a written one, the main problem of a verbal contract, in the event of a dispute, is establishing what exactly both parties had in mind.

Did the seller warrant the horse to be fit for hunting? If the seller agreed to the cost being paid in instalments, was there to be a reduction if the horse developed a certain ailment or failed to meet certain conditions? It is just such points as these which lead to conflict in a verbal contract as, human nature being what it is and both sides seeking to gain the maximum advantage for themselves, there is a natural tendency to play up those conditions which are advantageous to the case and play down or deny those which are not.

Provided all conditions are set down with simplicity and clarity, there can be no dispute over what was intended by either a warranty or condition of sale which has been reduced to writing, and this is of special importance if a horse is bought on approval. Consequently it is important that if an animal is purchased on a trial basis an agreement to purchase should be signed by all parties and the period of trial clearly stated. Such an agreement should give the purchase price and contain a warranty of soundness and a warranty of being free from vice.

This means that the seller, if not the actual owner of the animal, has the authority to sell. This may seem elementary but it has been known for people to sell horses they did not own due to dishonesty or because they thought, mistakenly, that they had the authority to do so.

It is, of course, a fundamental fact of all contracts that the seller has the right to sell and the buyer to receive what the law calls a good title to the property. If there is a defect in the seller's title and if the buyer acts before the defect is cured, if it can be, the buyer is entitled to repudiate the contract. In addition, the buyer is entitled to recover damages and if he has paid for the horse, the purchase price will form part of any damages claimed. If the buyer spent money in hiring a horsebox to transport the horse from Point A to Point B, and had other expenses in connection with the abortive sale, these, too, can be recovered by way of damages.

There is always the possibility that the defect in the seller's title can be corrected and if the buyer wishes to continue with the purchase, he can still claim damages for the breach of warranty of the seller's implied right to pass a good title: in other words, his right to sell the animal.

The person selling the horse is entitled to be paid at the time expressly stated or implied in the contract and in most cases this would be when the buyer takes possession of the horse, unless the animal has been sold on approval. Naturally, if the buyer fails to make payment at the agreed time, the seller has a right to sue for the money owed.

The time factor
One factor which may be of importance to any contract for the sale and purchase of a horse is time. For example, if the buyer tells the seller or the seller's agent that he wishes to take delivery of the horse on a certain date, he is not bound to accept delivery before that date.

On the other hand, if the owner of a riding school negotiated to buy a horse to expand his or her business during, say, school summer holidays and the horse was not delivered on the agreed date, the buyer might well be able to sustain a claim for damages because the seller was in breach of contract by not delivering the animal on the stated day. In such a circumstance the buyer must show that the seller could reasonably have foreseen that the buyer would suffer loss by non-delivery of the horse on the specified date. If the seller knew the buyer wanted the horse for a commercial purpose after the specified date of delivery he was clearly on notice that failure to deliver was likely to lead to a financial loss.

But suppose the buyer did not specify the reason for which the horse was required on a certain date. Could a claim for damages still be sustained? Much would depend on the buyer being able to demonstrate successfully that the seller could reasonably have foreseen that the horse was to be used for commercial purposes and that failure to perform the contract could lead to loss. If the purchaser had let the seller know, or the seller already knew, that he ran a riding school or livery stable from which horses were hired, it is more than likely that a judge would hold it reasonable for the seller to have foreseen the consequences of late delivery.

If the position is reversed and a buyer refuses to take delivery of a horse he has contracted to buy, the seller is entitled to seek damages for breach of contract. Just as the buyer has to do all he can to mitigate his damage which, in the case of the riding school or livery owner referred to above, is to try and get another horse as soon as possible, so, too, has the seller which, in this case, is to find another buyer for the horse. If he cannot, or if he fails to reach the price agreed with the buyer who has reneged on the deal, he is entitled to look to the buyer to make good the loss suffered and also the additional cost of stabling and feeding the horse until a new buyer is found.

Mistakes

There are other instances where the contract for the sale of a horse may be voided in certain circumstances. This is most likely to apply where there has been a mistake by one of the parties to the contract, which is known to the law as a unilateral mistake, or where there is a mistake by both parties, otherwise known as a bilateral mistake. A unilateral mistake could occur in the following example:

> Miss A agrees with Mr B to buy a horse in the mistaken belief that it has won prizes in dressage competitions and is capable of continuing to win such competitions. Mr B knows or ought to know that this is not so; and if this is the case, the contract to buy is voidable. This would not be the case if Mr B did not know that Miss A was mistaken in her belief.

In these circumstances the contract to buy will be rescinded or, if the seller asks a court for an order for specific performance – that is, the court ordering Miss A to go ahead and purchase the horse – such a request will be refused.

The next form of mistake to be considered is when both parties to a contract are mistaken. Where such a bilateral mistake occurs this can be subdivided into two distinct sections: an identical or common mistake and a non-identical or mutual mistake.

A common or identical mistake takes place when both buyer and seller have made a fundamental mistake about the contract, and would apply as follows:

> D owns a colt which he genuinely believes has been sired by a well-known show jumper. E wishes to buy D's colt because he too believes the colt to have been sired by the show jumper, so a price is agreed and the horse changes hands. Only later does E discover that the horse was not in fact sired by the show jumper. What, then, is his position in law?

Unless he can prove that D acted fraudulently or was guilty of misrepresentation, E has no comeback as the identical mistake – both D and E genuinely thinking the horse was sired by a show jumper – was common to both parties at the time the contract was entered into.

Where there is a mutual mistake which is not identical, the contract will not necessarily be declared void. The basis on which mutual mistake is laid is that both parties were mistaken about a fundamental fact but the mistakes were different. So if F, in selling a horse, puts a price on it because he thinks it has potential as a stallion and G agrees to pay the high price because he thinks it was sired by a well-known show jumper when, in fact, neither of these facts are correct, both sides are mistaken about the subject matter of the contract – the horse to be sold – although for different reasons.

In circumstances such as these, and if it is necessary to resort to litigation, a judge will seek to arrive at a conclusion which a reasonable man would come to, as far as the contract was concerned, as to the type of bargain both parties thought they had made. If this cannot be done the contract may be declared void for uncertainty.

Misrepresentation

Judging by the stories heard from time to time, many sellers are guilty of misrepresentation when it comes to describing a particular animal which is for sale. One of the most common misrepresentations is about age and it is not rare for an unsuspecting buyer to discover at a later date that an animal described as nine years old when purchased was, in fact, thirteen.

Obviously, both condition and age of a horse are important from the point of view of the buyer. The novice rider requires an animal which is docile, not one which has bad habits. A horse which is described as having been schooled over jumps will obviously fetch more money than one which is untrained. The variations are, in truth, endless but all play an important role in helping a potential buyer to make an offer for a particular animal.

In law a representation as to the fitness or ability of a horse is an inducement if it helps the would-be purchaser to decide to buy the animal, and a representation has to be a statement of a specific and existing fact, which can be verified, or of a past event. Consequently the age of a horse can certainly be verified and is very much an existing fact. To say a horse has been schooled over jumps or has won prizes at horse shows relates to past events.

It is not a misrepresentation to describe a horse as being capable of winning prizes at equestrian events or having potential as a stallion or brood-mare because this is a statement of opinion, unless it can be proved that the seller had no such opinion, which in most cases is difficult to do.

Furthermore, a line has to be drawn between a misrepresentaion and what is known as sales talk or puffing. This can be at times a fine line and in the event of a dispute the yardstick which a judge would use would be whether or not a reasonable man would be likely to take what a seller is saying as a puff for a particular horse, or a statement of fact.

Before going into the question of misrepresentation in greater depth it is necessary to look at what lies behind such a statement – which is what a representation, or misrepresentation, is. Put at its simplest, a statement has to be made in such a way that a buyer is induced to act upon it; thus the state of mind of both parties to the purchase is important. For the

16

seller a representation can be said to be the fact which clinches the deal; for the buyer, the fact which leads him to make up his mind to purchase that particular horse.

If the statement made by the seller is true, as when he says the horse has been schooled over jumps, all is well and good as no harm has been done and the buyer gets an animal which can take obstacles. If the animal has not been schooled over jumps this is a misrepresentation which induced the buyer to purchase a horse he would not otherwise have bought. In other words, a misrepresentation is something which affects the buyer's own judgement.

A misrepresentation need not be verbal or written: in certain circumstances, silence can be sufficient to establish a case. Just as saying that an actor performed to a half-full house sounds much better than saying the house was half empty, so too could a half truth be a misrepresentation provided that the person who receives the statement is intentionally given the wrong impression. For instance, if H correctly states to J that a horse he is selling is fit and J, uncertain as to whether he should buy or not, asks for time to think it over, returns a short time later and agrees to purchase, H would be guilty of a misrepresentation if, in the interim, the horse has developed or shown symptoms of a debilitating disease about which H keeps silent.

Misrepresentation is actionable in certain circumstances and much of the law is contained in the Misrepresentation Act 1967. The law recognises that there can be an innocent misrepresentation although it gives the other party the right to rescind the contract which has been induced by that misrepresentation. If a buyer has agreed to purchase an animal on the strength of an innocent misrepresentation but has not yet paid for it, that person is entitled to return the horse and call off the deal.

The seller in those circumstances would be ill advised to sue on the contract for specific performance – to ask a court to order the buyer to go ahead with the purchase – as the buyer can raise the innocent misrepresentation as a defence.

A buyer who finds himself in this position has to be careful of the manner in which he proceeds. He must not tell the seller that, despite the wrong statement, he will go ahead and buy the horse, and then at a later date change his mind. His decision to go ahead, despite knowing the truth about the particular horse, will be taken as affirming the contract to purchase. The buyer must also act as quickly as possible after discovering the truth about the horse. Failure to do so could well be held to be affirmation of the purchase.

Under Section 2(2) of the Misrepresentation Act, a court, in the case of innocent misrepresentation, may order that, instead of the contract being rescinded, damages should be awarded in lieu of rescission.

The next type of misrepresentation is the one which is made negligently and it is worth while taking a look at the legal meaning of what is a negligent misstatement. Such a misstatement or misrepresentation can be said to have been made when the circumstances are such that the person who made it was under a duty to exercise care and honesty, and a loss followed on the part of the person who acted upon the statement.

If the action for negligent misrepresentation is based on the contract which, where the sale of a horse is concerned, is almost certainly to be the case, Section 2(1) of the Misrepresentation Act provides that the person making the false statement is liable to pay damages unless he can prove he had reasonable grounds to believe, and did believe up to the time the contract was made, that the facts he represented were true. This, of course, puts the onus on the person making the statement. If damages are awarded for breach of the contract they will be limited to putting the buyer into the position he would have been in, but for the neglect misrepresentation, if he is unable to rescind the contract. The damages would cover the differences between the true value of the horse and the purchase price.

Fraudulent misrepresentation is best summed up as a false representation which the maker knows full well is untrue, or a statement made recklessly and without care as to whether it be true or not. In these cases the innocent party has several courses

18

of action open to him. He may affirm the purchase of the horse and then bring an action for the tort (wrong) of deceit; rescind the contract and sue for damages; or, if he has not taken possession of the horse, refuse to do so.

False statements or misrepresentations are also covered by the Trade Descriptions Act 1968 which applies to persons who are in business in the buying and selling of horses. Section 1(1) of the Act states:

> Any person who, in the course of a trade or business, applies a false trade description to any goods or supplies or offers to supply any goods to which a false trade description is applied, shall be guilty of an offence.

This means that any description of the horse, its abilities or age, during the course of a discussion between seller and potential buyer or in an advertisement, has to be true and accurate or the person making it is guilty of a criminal offence. On conviction for such an offence, a court is entitled to make an order against the convicted trader for compensation to be paid to the victim of the misdescription.

Buying a horse in partnership

It is not uncommon these days for two or more people to get together to buy a horse and although this can in some instances make economic sense, nevertheless it can cause greater problems than it sets out to overcome.

As far as the law is concerned it makes no difference whether one or a hundred and one people agree to buy a horse, a contract still exists. Nevertheless if two or three people decide to get together to purchase a horse it is essential that all owners are perfectly aware of the responsibility one has to the other. It is not a question of saying who owns what part of the animal: all partners in the agreement own the horse in equal shares unless there is an agreement to the contrary.

The law also takes the view that unless there is a partnership agreement which declares a contrary intention, all partners are equally liable for any debts incurred by the partners. Therefore it makes sound common sense, if two or more persons are getting together to buy a horse jointly, to sit down and work out the following points:

1 Is the animal to be owned in equal shares by all partners or are some to have a greater share than the others?
2 Does the person(s) with the greatest share also pay the greatest proportion of the costs of keeping the horse in livery, as well as bills for veterinary services, the services of a farrier or the provision of fodder?
3 In the event of the horse being sold, is the money split in equal shares or on a percentage basis commensurate with the amount of money each individual member put in?
4 What price should be paid if one member of the partnership wishes to sell his interest in the animal for any reason?

These are just some of the points which can and do arise when a horse is owned in partnership. How much more complicated, then, when one person either pays less towards the initial cost of purchasing the horse or less towards the upkeep of the animal, because that person can provide a stable or grazing free of charge. There are also the more basic matters such as who has the right to ride the horse at any particular time of the day, week, month or year.

It is obvious that unless a partnership is composed of persons so reasonable that they defer to each other at all times, acrimony can soon set in. If the law is invoked to resolve such a situation it can be an expensive affair asking a judge to determine what rights each partner has in the animal.

When the details of a prospective partnership have been agreed, and because of the value of horses today, it is worth while getting a partnership agreement drawn up by a solicitor. The fee for doing so should not be exorbitant provided that all the partners have done their homework in advance and come to a decision on all possible points.

It is interesting to note that the Jockey Club has recognised the problems which can arise with racehorses owned in partnerships. Rule 47 of the Rules of Racing holds all partners of a racehorse registered with the body liable jointly and severally for every stake, forfeit or fee and prohibits a partner from assigning all or part of his share without the permission of the other partners.

Racehorses can also be owned by syndicates although the Jockey Club limits the number of persons who can be members of such a syndicate to twelve. Even then the Club requires the legal possession of the horse to be vested in not less than three, or more than four, members of that syndicate.

A syndicate is different from a partnership. A partnership implies that all members are equal whereas with a syndicate not all members have to be equal. Some members may hold more shares than others. This is easy enough when dealing with a racehorse, as all that is really affected is the cost of purchase, training, upkeep, fees connected with racing the animal, etc, being apportioned in the same percentage as the shares owned by the individual members of the syndicate.

As far as the financial aspect is concerned, the same pattern can be followed by members of a syndicate which has bought a horse for leisure purposes. The problem will come in arriving at when and how often the members of the syndicate can ride the animal.

Whatever is decided, be it partnership or syndicate, these points should be reduced to writing and, if funds permit, the services of a solicitor used to draw up an agreement which will not lead to argument and discord at a later date.

Leasing

Leasing a horse for a specified or unspecified period of time is another way in which an animal can be obtained without the necessity of outright purchase. However, although this method may have merit in some circumstances it may, on the other hand, give rise to legal problems unless initial precautions are taken.

For the rider who wishes to compete in a number of events during the year but is without the necessary money to purchase a horse, leasing from an owner or stable might be the answer.

To all intents and purposes the animal is the property of the lessee, ie the person who has leased the animal from its owner.

If this is the case it is essential to draw up a lease agreement which will specify in the clearest of terms what are the responsibilities of the lessee. Such an agreement should state for how long the horse is being leased and how much the lessor – that is, the owner – is to receive.

A wise owner will certainly want to safeguard his animal and an agreement for a lease should contain other pertinent details: how and where is the horse to be stabled and what is the minimum standard of care?

An agreement to lease a horse should also contain clear indications that the owner expects the lessee to pay all veterinary expenses and the cost of the horse being properly and adequately shod, and state who is to be responsible for insuring the animal.

Perhaps the most contentious part of such an agreement is likely to be that which stipulates what the lessee may or may not do with the horse. If, for example, the horse is leased for show jumping or three-day eventing purposes, this should be stipulated in the most unambiguous manner possible. Without such precautions, in the eyes of the law the lessee is entitled to use the horse for any purpose during the life of the lease.

An analogous situation is the leasing of a flat: under such a lease the landlord gives the lessee the right of occupation and enjoyment of the flat but is most likely to stipulate that the premises be used for residential purposes only. If this is not stated, then, subject to planning regulations, the lessee could, if he wished, use the premises for commercial purposes. So it is with a horse: without inserting restrictions into the lease agreement there is nothing to stop the lessee making commercial use of the animal by renting it out to casual users, with possible disastrous results as far as the horse is concerned.

Perhaps the most important matter to be included in any lease is the question of insurance. Normally the person leasing the horse should be expected to bear this cost, although it is for the parties to the leasing agreement to decide between themselves. This is a matter which should not be overlooked; it is not unreasonable for the lessee to expect the lessor to have insured the animal and if the agreement is silent on this point, a court will inevitably come to the same conclusion.

Once an owner has entered into a leasing agreement he has no control over the horse until the period of time under the lease has expired. Although the lessee has possession of the horse he does not, of course, have ownership although his possession gives him all the rights of ownership save that of disposing of the animal, subject to the terms of the lease being observed.

Thus a lessee who fails to observe the terms of the lease may find the owner demanding the return of the animal. If, as a result of the lessee's failure to observe the terms and conditions, the value of the horse has diminished, the owner can claim damages for that amount.

Lending or borrowing a horse

All that has been written so far in this chapter on buying or leasing a horse has fundamentally been based on the law of contract, with the underlying assumption that both parties were entering into a contractual relationship. In the case of buying a horse it is agreed that the owner wishes to dispose of it and that the buyer will provide what the law knows as consideration, ie money or money's worth. In the case of a horse which is leased, in return for possession and use of the horse for a given period of time, the lessee agrees to certain conditions which inevitably include some form of payment, even if it is only the assumption of the cost of livery, insurance, etc.

But when a horse is loaned different considerations apply and the first and most crucially important point to be established is whether or not the owner and the borrower intend to establish a legal relationship of a contractual form.

If the owner lends his horse to a friend for an afternoon's riding or a day's hunting, it is highly unlikely that in their minds there is any intention to enter into a contractual relationship and without the meeting of minds there can be no contract. So if a horse is lent in such circumstances, or for any

23

other reason, and meets with an accident, there can be no come-back for the owner on the grounds of negligent performance of a contract although there might be a claim in tort for negligent handling of the animal if this was the case.

Again, by the very nature of the generally accepted meaning of the words to lend or to borrow, no consideration is implied and without consideration there can be no contract. On the other hand, if the owner of a horse lends the animal to a friend for whatever length of time and the friend in return agrees to let the owner have use of his car or caravan for a holiday in the future, a contract exists. It is not necessary for money to be involved as long as there is consideration and in the example cited above, consideration is the use of the car or caravan.

If a horse is lent to another with no payment of any kind it is still essential that there should be a memorandum of agreement between owner and borrower – if only to state that the borrower accepts responsibility for any damage which might result from his use of the horse and undertakes to look after the animal which, of course, implies that it will be properly stabled and fed. If the thought of entering into a legal agreement is anathema to both parties, there should still be some forum in case of a future dispute and it could well be that any loan agreement should include a clause for the appointment of an arbitrator in the event of a dispute. It cannot be stressed too much how important it is in any agreement, whether the parties to it intend to create legal relations or not, for details to be put in writing, thus avoiding misunderstanding and contention at a later date.

Importing horses
Horses are not solely purchased in this country; indeed, many of our finest racehorses are bought in such sales as Keeneland in Kentucky and the Curragh in the Republic of Ireland, and even animals of much less distinguished lineage may be bought abroad. If this is the case a licence is needed under the Importation of Equine Animals Order 1979 to bring into this country horses or ponies purchased in Europe (with the

exception of France and Ireland), Australia, New Zealand, Japan and the continent of America. Anyone thinking of bringing in a horse from those areas for which an import licence is needed should not make any arrangements until the licence is granted. The necessary form can be obtained from either the Ministry of Agriculture, Fisheries and Food, the Department of Agriculture and Fisheries for Scotland or the Welsh Office Agriculture Department.

The form is comparatively simple: persons wishing to import a horse into this country have to give particulars of its name, age, colour, sex and breed, as well as answering a number of questions. These include naming the country from which it is being imported, the date of importation and the proposed travel route and, in declaring this route, all ports and airports either the vessel or aircraft carrying the horse stops at en route to Great Britain must be listed.

It is also necessary to list not only the full address of where the horse is currently located but, if this should be the case, all countries with appropriate dates where the horse has been within the preceding six months. If the animal comes from the United States of America it is necessary to declare whether or not it has been vaccinated against Venezuelan equine encephalomyelitis (VEE), as it will not be allowed into this country until at least fourteen days after vaccination. The address of where in this country the horse or horses are to be sent must also be given, as must the name of the owner or person in charge of the importation.

No animal which has been in any country in the continent of America, other than the USA, Mexico, Canada, Jamaica, Bermuda, Argentina, Uruguay, Paraguay, Chile or that part of Brazil which lies south of the River Amazon, during the three months previous to importation will be accepted. Furthermore, no horse will be accepted which, in the six months prior to importation, has been in any country where African horse sickness has occurred during the previous two years or where vaccination against the disease has been practised during the previous two years.

25

CONTRACT OF SALE

The seller .... of ....
....
The buyer ....of ....
....
In consideration of the sum of £ .... today received
by the Seller from the Buyer, the Seller transfers ownership of
the

....

                           (1) named ... to the Buyer
                           and

warrants that the said horse is free from vice and fit for quiet
riding .... (2)
It is agreed that if the said horse does not comply with any
warranty herein contained the Buyer must return it to the Seller
at his address shown herein not later than .... (3) days from
the date hereof accompied by a certificate of and signed by a
qualified veterinary surgeon specifying in what respect the horse
does not comply. In the event of a dispute as to compliance with
any such warranty the horse shall be referred to a qualified
veterinary surgeon to be agreed upon by the parties hereto or
failing such an agreement nominated by ....
The decision of such veterinary surgeons or arbitrator shall be
binding on the parties hereto.
As witness the hands of the parties have this .... 198........(4)
Signed by the seller in the).. (5)
presence of).. (6)
Signed by the Buyer in the).. (5)
presence of).. (6)

Notes

(1) Brief description of horse eg 'grey hunter'.
(2) Specify any exceptions or qualifications to the warranty; eg
    'except that he shies at loud or sudden noise' or any
    additional warranties given.
(3) State the number of days within which the horse must be
    returned. Seven days would usually be the maximum.

(4) Insert the actual date of the agreement.

(5) Seller's and buyer's signatures respectively.

(6) Witness should sign here and insert his/her address and occupation.

General: (a) This agreement should be signed by both parties in duplicate so that each has a copy for future reference and it is recommended that a certificate by a qualified veterinary surgeon should be obtained by the buyer before entering into any agreement.

(b) This agreement is suitable for the usual sale and purchase of a horse for riding. However, if there are special circumstances or exceptional warranties, you should take specialist advice or have the agreement drawn up by your solicitor.

If the horse to be imported is a British racehorse or show or competition horse returning home, the date of its export from this country must be given, as must the name and place of the event in which the animal has competed. Similarly, in the case of a horse being imported to this country to race or compete, the name, place and date of the event must be given, as must the duration of the proposed stay.

Auction sales

No one should buy a horse at an auction sale before first inspecting the animals offered, as the consumer safeguards under the Sale of Goods Act (See Chapter 2) do *not* apply to auctions.

Sales at an auction are binding from the moment the auctioneer brings down his hammer. Before that time a bidder may withdraw his bid. It is not unusual at an auction sale for a horse to be entered at a reserve price. This price is not known to the public attending the auction and if it is not reached the item will be withdrawn.

There have been occasions when auctioneers have mistakenly knocked down an item at a price below the reserve. Unlike the normal law of contract for sales, even though the buyer may think the deal has been concluded with the acceptance of his bid by the auctioneer, the seller is within his rights to abort the sale as the item has not reached its reserve price.

After a bid has been accepted at an auction, the method of payment and the time when it is due may often be subject to conditions attached to that particular auction, so potential buyers should be familiar with such details before bidding.

It is essential that a buyer who does not take immediate possession of the particular horse or pony purchased should agree with the seller that the price will be paid and ownership pass from seller to buyer when the buyer takes possession. It must be remembered that possession of a horse does not necessarily equate with ownership or even payment of the price in some circumstances. The reason for this is that, in English law, ownership usually passes from seller to buyer when an agreement to purchase is finalised, even if the buyer does not take physical possession of his purchase.

If the owner does not take possession and arranges for delivery of the horse within a specified time, and the animal dies or is seriously injured, the purchaser is still responsible for paying the seller, if he has not already done so, and ownership has passed. Consequently, it is of enormous importance that when a horse is purchased but not taken possession of, it should be stated in any contract for sale that ownership will not pass until safe delivery of the animal to the buyer is made.

2 THE SALE OF GOODS ACT (1979)

A horse dealer sells a horse which he says
is fit for jumping without further training.
In fact it is not.

A saddler recommends a particular
saddle as being ideal for a specific
purpose. It is not.

The Sale of Goods Act gives the buyer
protection in both cases.

The Sale of Goods Act 1979 protects consumers but as far as purchasers of horses and related equipment are concerned is limited to only those who buy from horse dealers or from businesses who trade in a retail capacity, although a person who buys directly from a manufacturer is also protected by the Act. In both the instances quoted on page 29, the purchaser would be protected by the provisions of the Act but it must be stressed that the whole basis of the Act is that of contract. Nevertheless, although the initial transaction may be a simple contract, the Act, as will be seen in the following pages, deal with a great many aspects.

The definition of a contract of sale of goods as defined under the Sale of Goods Act 1979, Section 2 reads:

A contract of sale of goods is a contract by which the seller transfers or agrees to transfer the property in goods to the buyer for a money consideration called the price. There may be a contract of sale between one part owner and another;
Where under a contract of sale the transfer of property in the goods is to take place at a future time or subject to some condition later to be fulfilled the contract is called an agreement to sell;
An agreement to sell becomes a sale when the time elapses or the conditions are fulfilled subject to which the property in the goods is to be transferred.

It will be seen that the definition of a contract of sale refers to 'property', which although the word 'sale' appears in the title of the Act. Property in this sense must be taken to mean that the seller is in a position to give the buyer the legal title to the goods. It must always be kept in mind that physical possession cannot be equated with ownership as such. Only a person with a legal right to sell can pass a good title and thereby transfer ownership. For this reason the purchase of goods on hire purchase does not transfer ownership of the goods in question because until the end of the agreement the goods belong to the hire purchase company financing the transaction. When the agreement ends, and subject to all payments having been met, it is then necessary for the purchaser to pay a further amount – usually a nominal sum of one pound – to buy the goods and have legal ownership.

Another point worth noting in the definitions is the use of the word 'money', which makes it clear beyond doubt that any other form of purchase – such as a barter – is *not* covered by the Act although a transaction in which goods are accepted in part exchange is covered.

It is also essential that the goods to be purchased should be specifically identified and this can be of great importance if articles are bought by mail order, or even if a verbal order is placed without the goods being identified. A good example of this is if the reader of a mail order catalogue or an advertisement orders 'a riding jacket'. If only one such jacket is available in the advertisement or catalogue, this should be specific enough, but if more than one riding jacket is on offer there is uncertainty; so it may be said that the contract cannot be fulfilled because of the buyer's failure to specify what jacket is required.

An important part of the Act is Section 20, because a person can pay the full asking price for a horse and receive a bill of sale which, in effect, transfers the property and legal title to the buyer, and then, for a variety of good reasons, be unable to take the horse with him at the time the transaction is completed. If the horse remains with the seller until it can be transported to the buyer, who is at risk if anything happens to the horse before what might be called physical possession passes into the hands of the buyer?

Section 20(1) of the Act reads:

> Unless otherwise agreed, the goods remain at the seller's risk until the property in them is transferred to the buyer, but when the property in them is transferred to the buyer the goods are at the buyer's risk, whether delivery has been made or not.

There is no need to stress the importance of this point, especially if the goods in question should be a horse. In circumstances such as these, the sensible purchaser will either write into a contract of sale that the risk remains with the seller while the horse is in his possession, or take out immediate insurance himself. Real life, however, is never as clear cut and uncomplicated as this, and the following situation could arise:

31

A agrees to buy a seven-year-old brown gelding for £2,000 from B, who is a recognised horse dealer. The payment is by cheque and the arrangement is that, after allowing four working days for the cheque to clear, A will send a horse box to pick up his horse. For reasons which have nothing to do with B, A fails to send a horse box on the appointed day and unfortunately the horse sustains injury when he casts himself in his stable. Who suffers the loss?

To answer this as far as the Act is concerned it is necessary to look at Section 20(2) which reads:

But where delivery has been delayed through the fault of either buyer or seller the goods are at the risk of the party at fault as regards any loss which might not have occurred but for such fault.

In this example, had A arranged for the horse box to arrive on time the horse he purchased would not have cast itself in its stable; so A is at fault and must bear the loss. If, however, B had arranged to have the horse transported to A as soon as the cheque had cleared and was at fault for not doing so, the loss would have fallen on him.

A similar situation can arise over the sale of hay which may be purchased and left in a field to await either delivery or collection. Fodder can be destroyed by fire or ruined by sudden torrential rain.

Both of these examples raise a fine point: when was the property transferred from seller to buyer? Remember that possession does not constitute ownership. Bearing in mind that a contract for the sale of goods is completed under the definitions contained in Section 2, it may be that the property has passed when its agreed purchase price has been met – and this applies whether or not the property remains for whatever reason in the physical possession of the seller.

The prudent purchaser will look to Section 2(5) which reads:

Where under a contract of sale the transfer of the property in the goods is to take place at a future time or subject to some condition later to be fulfilled the contract is called an agreement to sell.

The person wishing to buy a horse or a large amount of fodder for which he is unable to arrange immediate delivery can best protect his interests by entering into an agreement to sell, with the condition to be fulfilled before the contract is completed being the safe delivery of whatever was ordered. Failure to effect safe delivery would render the agreement unenforceable as the seller would not have carried out his responsibilities in accordance with agreed terms. This may seem a cumbersome way in which to purchase goods but where a substantial sum of money is involved the loss can be quite disastrous.

There are, of course, circumstances in an agreement to sell where, through no fault on either side, the articles to be purchased are destroyed before property changes hands. In these circumstances the contract is said to be frustrated. This is a common law concept which holds that a contract is considered to be incapable of performance if an event strikes at the very root of the contract – such as fodder being destroyed by fire or water, or a horse meeting with a fatal accident – and beyond what was in the minds of the parties involved. The Law Reform (Frustrated Contracts) Act 1943 laid down that, subject to certain provisions, all monies paid under a contract which had become frustrated were recoverable and any money due was not payable. The exceptions are where the contract itself has a clause to cover frustration, a contract of insurance or the carriage of goods by sea, or a contract not governed by English law.

Section 7 of the Sale of Goods Act 1979 provides protection for the buyer of specific goods which may perish:

> Where there is an agreement to sell specific goods and subsequently the goods, without any fault on the part of the seller or buyer, perish before the risk passes to the buyer, the agreement is avoided.

In view of this it may be thought unnecessary to rely on an agreement to sell with the condition that the goods be safely delivered as previously suggested. This may well be the case, but it must be pointed out that if either buyer or seller wish to rely on Section 7 of the Act the goods have to have been specified. This is easy in the case of a horse which, hopefully, would never be purchased sight unseen; but this is not always the case with fodder, which may not be specified when ordered.

It could be that an order is placed for a ton of hay to be delivered when ready. This would obviously be unspecified. On the other hand, an order of a ton of hay now in the Dutch barn belonging to Farmer A is in respect of specified goods.

So far this chapter has dealt with the situation which might arise before the property in the goods has passed to the buyer by his taking delivery. The question of delivery is dealt with in Section 32(1) of the Act, which reads:

> Where, in pursuance of a contract of sale, the seller is authorised or required to send the goods to the buyer, delivery of the goods to a carrier (whether named by the buyer or not) for the purpose of transmission to the buyer is prima facie deemed to be delivery of goods to the buyer.

Academic writer's have put forward a number of logical arguments on what is meant by the phrase 'authorised or required to send the goods to the buyer' and even on what is meant by a carrier. But it is only necessary here to emphasise the importance, if anything is to be delivered, of precise, unambiguous wording of any agreement so to do. To avoid argument it is advisable to stipulate in such an agreement whether or not the seller, or a carrier appointed by him, is to deliver the goods, or whether a carrier is to be authorised by the buyer to collect and deliver.

If the seller delivers then he is, of course, his own agent so the property can be said not to have passed to the buyer. On the other hand if the seller of a horse handed over the animal to a firm of horse transporters this would constitute delivery and the passing of the property; and the same would apply, of course, if the buyer engaged the service of a transport firm to pick up the horse.

Buyers who are relying on goods being delivered to them should be aware that it is essential for them to determine to their own satisfaction when they in fact are deemed under the Act to have taken delivery. They must also make absolutely certain that the carrier, whether it be themselves or an independent firm, has sufficient insurance cover to meet any possible loss

34

which might occur while the goods are in transit.

Nevertheless, the Act does give some protection to the buyer as far as delivery is concerned, as will be seen from Section 32(2), which states:

> Unless otherwise authorised by the buyer, the seller must make such contract with the carrier on behalf of the buyer as may be reasonable having regard to the nature of the goods and the other circumstances of the case; and if the seller omits to do so, and the goods are lost or damaged in the course of transit, the buyer may decline to treat the delivery to the carrier as delivery to himself or may hold the seller responsible in damages.

This sub-section is really enshrining common sense into the legislation by saying that proper forms of transportation must be used for the particular items being carried. So a horse dealer who undertakes to deliver an animal must use either a horse transporter or trailer as these are the only appropriate and safe vehicles.

The word 'delivery', as will have been seen, features large in the Act and, again, Section 27 has something to say on the subject:

> It is the duty of the seller to deliver the goods, and of the buyer to accept and pay for them in accordance with the terms of the contract of sale.

Delivery in this sense does not always mean that the seller physically delivers the goods to the buyer although as far as the sale of a horse or a large quantity of fodder is concerned, this may well be the case.

The Act, in Section 61(1), defines delivery as the voluntary transfer of possession from one person to another, while Section 28 lays upon the buyer the obligation to pay for the goods if he has not already done so.

As far as the Act is concerned, goods supplied on approval or on sale or return terms are dealt with under Section 18, which states, *inter alia*:

When goods are delivered to the buyer on approval or on sale or return or other similar terms the property in the goods passes to the buyer:
(a) when he signifies his approval or acceptance to the seller or does any other act adopting the transaction; (b) if he does not signify his approval or acceptance to the seller but retains the goods without giving notice of rejection, then, if a time has been fixed for the return of the goods, on the expiration of that time, and, if no time has been fixed, on the expiration of a reasonable time.

For a start it must be remembered that the person accepting a horse, or any other item come to that, on approval or sale or return, does not have the property in the particular item transferred to him. He is actually what the law terms a bailee, ie a person holding goods on behalf of another. He becomes the owner when he tells the seller that he wishes to purchase the horse and pays the asking price or 'does any other act adopting the transaction'. One such act would be having a colt gelded, for it can be argued with great force that only the owner of a horse should and/or could have the operation undertaken. Another act would be to enter the horse in an equestrian event in his own name and not that of the seller.

The second part of the section quoted above must be considered in two parts. The first – 'if he does not signify his approval or acceptance to the seller but retains the goods without giving notice of rejection' – needs no explanation for at the end of the specified period of having a horse on approval, silence may well be construed as acceptance.

The second part – 'if no time has been fixed, on the expiration of a reasonable time' – needs a little more explanation. Although it is doubtful if any dealer would let a horse go on approval without specifying a time limit, the possibility does exist, and what is a reasonable time is matter of argument. If the would-be purchaser wishes to use a horse for competitions before coming to a decision, a whole season may be held to be a reasonable time. If the custom of the trade for a horse to be out on approval is for no more than one month, a judge would probably hold this to be a reasonable time.

In the absence of a contract of sale or an agreement to sell, a person holding goods on approval would not be responsible for loss or destruction if such damage was not his fault. This would apply only if the particular individual had taken any action which indicated he was prepared to enter into a contract of sale or an agreement to purchase.

However, if the person having the horse on approval fails to take care of the animal, and it is damaged or even killed, that person is liable, as any bailee would be, for the reduced value or total loss of the animal. This presupposes that there has been no arrangement for the risk to remain with the would-be seller, unlikely though the chances of this happening may be. Indeed, it is far more likely that one of the terms of having the horse on approval would be that the prospective buyer should take out adequate insurance. (As mentioned earlier, the Act does not apply to sales arranged between private individuals but only where the seller is in business. A private agreement for a potential buyer to have a horse on approval should always specify the length of time involved and who is to be responsible should the horse meet with an accident or need veterinary attention.)

The Sale of Goods Act is a massive piece of legislation, to say the least, and so far references to various sections of the Act have been made only as far as they are likely to affect the sale, transit and delivery of horses and fodder although they do, of course, apply with equal force to other articles. The selection of those sections must be a subjective one as far as this book is concerned, although nearly every section could be said to apply: but if each was examined and commented upon, there would be little or no room here for any other topic.

Nevertheless, there are three sections which can be described without exaggeration as the cornerstone of consumer law and which apply to all those buying goods through retail outlets or, in the case of horses and ponies, from dealers. Before considering in some detail how these three sections – 13, 14 and 15 – apply, it is helpful to look at Section 12. This is a long section which can best be paraphrased by saying that in a contract of sale there is an implied condition that the seller has

37

the right to sell the goods, and in the case of an agreement for sale he will have such a right when the time comes for the property to pass to the buyer. It can be argued that this must surely always be the case. In a perfect world this would be so, but it must be remembered that a person in possession of a horse may not be the owner and therefore has no right to sell. There are also circumstances where a genuine mis-understanding between owner and the person in possession of an animal could result in the horse being sold by the person in possession – the bailee – without the approval of the owner.

If it is implied under Section 12 of the Act that the seller has the right to sell, Sections 13, 14 and 15 imply three major factors in all contracts for sale of goods made by a person in the course of business.

Section 13 reads:

Sale by description.
(1) Where there is a contract for the sale of goods by description, there is an implied condition that the goods will correspond with the description.

There are other sub-sections concerning this point but for the purpose of this book the above quoted will suffice and it really means exactly what it says, that the goods must match the description. For example, if a horse dealer describes an animal to an eventual buyer as being nine years of age and this is not the case, the horse is not as described and the buyer can claim against the seller under the Act. Similarly, if the owner of a horse bought from a forage merchant a supplementary feed for a horse which was described, either in writing or orally, as containing certain ingredients and/or vitamins, and all or just one are found on analysis to be absent, again the goods are not as described.

Perhaps this section might apply mainly to the purchase of riding habit. Consequently, a riding mackintosh described as rainproof must be just that; it might be showerproof, but that is not enough within the strict provisions of Section 13 of the Act. This even applies to colour; for instance if a riding jacket bought by mail order is described as brown and the one received is a different colour, although in such circumstances the seller would rapidly put things right.

Misdescriptions can, in some circumstances, be a breach of the Trade Descriptions Act 1968, of which more later.

Section 14 reads, *inter alia*:

> Where the seller sells goods in the course of a business, there is an implied condition that the goods supplied under the contract are of merchantable quality, except that there is no such condition:
> (a) as regards defects specifically drawn to the buyer's attention before the contract is made; or
> (b) if the buyer examines the goods before the contract is made, as regards defects which that examination ought to reveal.

Although this section does not specifically refer to an agreement for sale, which features in earlier sections of the Act and is referred to at the beginning of this chapter, academic lawyers take the view that this is understood to be included. If this was not the case, it would make a nonsense of a major plank of today's consumer law.

Before the 1979 Act, judges over the years since the passing of the 1893 Act of the same name, had come up with a number of definitions of what was or was not merchantable quality. The 1979 Act, however, overcame this problem by stating in Section 14(6):

> . . . Goods of any kind are of merchantable quality . . . if they are fit for the purpose or purposes for which goods of that kind are commonly bought as it is reasonable to expect having regard to any description applied to them, the price (if relevant) and all other relevant circumstances.

Some may think that this statutory description is itself amorphous but it is not difficult to apply the various component parts to relevant circumstances likely to affect the purchase of horses or ponies.

To go back to the earlier part of Section 14; readers will note the reference to defects specifically drawn to the buyer's attention before the contract of sale is agreed. This underlines the necessity of inspecting all goods, let alone horses, before purchase, and is really a simple proposition. If a buyer inspecting a horse notices some physical defect which might affect its stamina or ability and chooses to go ahead with the purchase either at the price asked, or at a reduced price as a result of bargaining and bringing into account the obvious defect, there can be no claim.

The term 'fitness for purpose' appears twice in Section 14 of the Act. In Section 14(3) it is used in connection with goods being required for a particular purpose. Consequently a buyer who requires a horse specifically for jumping, or a waterproof riding coat, and has made the seller aware of his particular needs, will have the protection of the Act if he is sold inappropriate goods.

On the other hand, under Section 14(6) the goods must be fit and of merchantable quality for their normal purpose. So it becomes a matter of argument as to whether or not a person buying a horse, without saying it was required for jumping, could claim that its inability to take obstacles afforded the buyer protection under this particular section. In other words, would it be held that jumping was a purpose for which a horse was normally bought? And whereas a riding coat might be suitable for some purposes, for it to be suitable for riding in rain it would have to be waterproof.

These are matters open to both opinion and argument, and it is impossible to be dogmatic about the topic: sufficient to say that much would depend on the particular facts of each individual case. It is absolutely no use buying a horse which has been used only for gentle canters across flat countryside and expecting it to be hunted without mishap or entered for equestrian events without training, and then blaming the seller for its shortcomings. Unless he knew the horse was to be used immediately for hunting or eventing, how can he be blamed?

A seller cannot be held responsible under the 'fitness for purpose' condition in Section 14(3) if a horse sold specifically for an adult to ride proves difficult for a child to handle. On the other hand, a seller *would* be responsible if, on being told the buyer wanted a horse which a child could ride with ease, he sold one which could be ridden safely only by an adult. The same

principle applies to riding equipment and clothing, always
provided that the articles are put to their normal use and not for
something for which they are totally unsuitable.

The phrase referring to price in Section 14(6) is also
important, for there the legislation is recognising a fundamental
fact: that normally a buyer gets exactly what he pays for. If a
buyer pays a ridiculously low price for a horse which is useless
except as a stable companion, then in any subsequent legal
dispute the price would be an important factor in determining
whether or not the seller was in breach of Section 14.

The section also covers second-hand goods and those which
are 'seconds' – manufacturer's rejects. A buyer of such goods
cannot expect top quality, although that does not necessarily
mean that it will not be received.

What can be described as a catch-all phrase is the reference to
'all other relevant circumstances', and this would include what
is customary for usage for the goods in question.

Section 15 of the Act is most likely to apply to owners of
livery stables, riding schools and those fortunate enough to
have their own stabling and/or grazing and who buy fodder in
bulk. This section reads, *inter alia*:

(1) A contract of sale is a contract of sale by sample when there is an
express or implied term in the contract
(2) In the case of a contract for sale by sample there is an implied
condition
(a) that the bulk will correspond to the sample in quality;
(b) that the buyer will have a reasonable opportunity of comparing
the bulk with the sample;
(c) that the goods will be free from any defect, rendering them
unmerchantable, which would not be apparent on reasonable
examination of the sample.

A person may obtain a sample bale of good quality hay from a
forage-merchant and, on the strength of the quality of the
sample, place an order for, say, a ton of the same hay. Under
Section 15, the buyer is protected if the bulk order does not
match in quality the fodder he received as a sample. Sub-
sections 2(b) and 2(c) need no explanation.

Exclusion clauses

Prior to the boom in growth of consumer law in the 1960s and 1970s it was not uncommon for what are called exclusion or exemption clauses to appear in contracts of sale. These clauses sought to exempt the manufacturers and sellers for any liability as far as merchantable quality, etc, was concerned if the goods were in any way defective or inferior. Although these clauses were frowned upon by the courts, who interpreted them rigidly and in many cases against suppliers, etc, who sought to hide behind them, it was not until the Supply of Goods (Implied Terms) Act 1973 was passed that Parliament took a positive step to protect consumers and this has been built into the 1979 Act.

As a result of the 1973 Act, liability for a seller's implied undertaking to pass a good title to the goods cannot be restricted or excluded by reference to any term of the contract. Nor can the seller seek to limit, as far as a consumer is concerned, the undertaking that the goods comply with either description or sample and that they are of merchantable quality and fit for their particular purpose.

There is a further item of legislation – the Unfair Contract Terms Act 1977 – which bans any contract from seeking to exclude liability for death or injury and will only allow a person to shelter behind an exclusion clause denying liability for damage, etc, if it is reasonable in all the circumstances. But it must be remembered that this particular Act, like the Sale of Goods Act 1979, applies only when the seller is in business as retailer or supplier, and not to private transactions.

Obviously this is a crucial piece of legislation offering protection to the buyer who purchases goods from a retailer or a seller such as a horse dealer. Any horse dealer who sought in a bill of sale to exclude liability for death or injury caused through the behaviour of a mean or high-spirited horse would be unable to do so.

The Unfair Contract Terms Act 1977 went a step further in consumer protection as it made it unlawful for a supplier of *services* to shelter behind an exclusion or exemption clause unless it was reasonable in all the circumstances. What could be termed reasonable in all the circumstances cannot be simply defined as each case has to be examined and dealt with on its own merits or demerits. Nevertheless, it is worth examining a hypothetical case to give some indication of how the law under this particular Act might be applied.

Miss A wishes to transport her horse from its stable to a gymkhana in which she is taking part some distance away. She engages the services of a local firm of horse transporters and signs a standard form of agreement which on the reverse contains, among the conditions of transporation, an exclusion clause exempting the transport company from liability for any action which might cause the death of, or injury to, a horse being transported.

On the way to the gymkhana, through the negligence of the driver of the transporter, the horse is injured with the result that Miss A has to pay several hundred pounds in veterinary fees.

She later sues the firm of transport contractors for damages and the firm points out that in its conditions of carriage there is a clause exempting it from liability for any damage whether caused by the negligence of its servants or not.

Miss A argues that she was not aware of that particular condition and even if she had been it was unreasonable within the meaning of the Act. As far as Miss A's claim to be ignorant of the condition is concerned, she would have no case as the law presumes that when a person is of full contractual capacity – ie, over the age of 18 and in full possession of their faculties and not induced to enter into a contract by duress or fraudulent means – he or she has read the contract and by signing it so acknowledges. (It would be different if the exclusion clause was contained in any receipt given after signing the contract or brought to her notice after any such contract had been signed, and in such cases protection would not have to be sought from the Unfair Contract Terms Act.)

Miss A would have to prove that the exclusion clause was unreasonable in the circumstances, and in this instance much would depend on the bargaining power of the transport contractors *vis-à-vis* Miss A. If Miss A could prove that the particular firm of transport contractors was the only one within a reasonable distance of where her horse was stabled and, as such, the firm used what might be described as its local monopoly power on a take it or leave it basis, it is probable that a court would hold the exclusion clause to be unreasonable in the circumstances. It would be most unlikely that a court would expect Miss A to shop around and add to the expense by getting another firm some distance from where her horse was stabled, and who did not seek to exclude liability, to undertake the job.

If, on the other hand, there were a number of firms in Miss A's neighbourhood who would have undertaken the job without seeking to exclude liability, a court might hold that although the exemption clause was unreasonable, it was not so in *all* the circumstances as Miss A could have made alternative arrangements. The reverse would almost undoubtedly apply if there were a number of transport contractors in Miss A's neighbourhood and all of them included exemption clauses in their contracts. Then there would be a high degree of probability that the exclusion clause of the firm used by Miss A would be held to be unreasonable and the firm would be liable for damages.

Guarantees

Guarantees might be given by manufacturers in respect of goods such as tack, riding clothes and stable equipment which are necessary parts of owning and/or riding horses. Are they of any use?

It all depends on what use is made of the guarantee. Guarantees under which the manufacturer makes good any defects which are not caused by fair wear and tear or misuse during a period of time – usually the first twelve months after purchase – are worth while in as much as they ensure that the repair is carried out by those with the appropriate skill and training, and that any replacement parts used are the correct ones.

Nevertheless, in law no contractual relationship exists between the ultimate buyer and the maker if the particular article is sold, as it invariably is, through a retail outlet.

Retailers, of course, are in favour of guarantees, which enable them to pass on to the manufacturer the responsibility they owe to their customers for faulty goods. However, in law retailers are, as we have seen earlier in this chapter, responsible for making good any loss buyers suffer as a result of purchasing articles which are not of merchantable quality or fit for their purpose.

Consequently, the wise buyer who is aware of his or her rights will insist on remedial action being taken by the retailer with whom he or she has been in a contractual relationship. It must be pointed out that the customer is not obliged to accept a credit note, nor is the retailer obliged to replace the defective article. All the customer can insist on is that the purchase price be refunded, although if injury or damage has been caused as a result of faulty equipment, damages can be claimed as well. This may be thought to be exceedingly harsh on a trader who sold an article which to him was in first-class condition, but the retailer has redress under the Sale of Goods Act against the manufacturer.

Retailers are not obliged to refund money for any reason other than for goods which are not of merchantable quality. The fact that so many do, if the buyer decides the goods are the wrong sort or, on reflection, that he cannot afford them, is a gesture of good consumer relations on the part of retailers rather than any legal obligation.

Trades descriptions

The first chapter of this book has dealt with the buying of a horse with reference mainly to the Misrepresentation Act 1967 under which the buyer may seek recourse from a *private* seller of a horse which is not what was claimed by the seller on its behalf. So far this chapter has dealt with the legal provisions which protect the buyer from the person who sells horses or goods as a business, although it must always be remembered that the law is not all one way and in favour of the consumer. There is always the overriding consideration that unless the supplier has been at fault there is the obligation on the purchaser to accept delivery and pay for his or her purchase.

So far, the various Acts of Parliament which have been examined in this book involve the dissatisfied consumer invoking the civil law and initiating a civil action on his or her own behalf. The Trade Descriptions Act 1967 invokes the criminal law on behalf of a dissatisfied consumer and is enforced by the Trading Standards departments of local authorities to whom consumer complaint should be made. Under this Act false descriptions and statements about goods and services which are offered in the course of business or trade are criminal offences, as are indications as to price which are misleading or downright false.

A person whose business is dealing with horses would be in breach of the Act if he described a horse in any way which was false, for instance if he tried to pass on a horse as being fully trained in such disciplines as dressage or jumping when it was not. Obviously the Act would be breached if a dealer made a false statement about a horse's age and, possibly, its state of health. The qualification of possibility is used because expression of opinion is not necessarily the same as a false statement. It is arguable that a buyer should not rely on a seller's statement about the health of a horse because this is something which calls for the specialist and professional knowledge of a veterinary surgeon.

What is known as 'trade puffing' need not necessarily be a false description. If a horse dealer categorically described an animal as one which had won point to point races, had stamina and good finishing speed, when it turned out to be patently untrue, this would be a false description whether or not the buyer wanted the horse for racing. On the other hand, to say of a horse that 'he goes like the wind' is a piece of hyperbole not meant to be taken seriously.

Conversely, a horse dealer would be committing an offence under the Act if he told the owner of a horse which was being offered to him for sale that the horse was really not fit for anything but, out of the goodness of his heart, he would give the owner £50 for it instead of the £500 being asked. (No offence would be committed under the Act if the owner was selling the horse to a private buyer who made the same statement.)

The same legislation applies to buying equipment. If a trader wrongly describes the goods an offence is committed under the Act. Such false descriptions can apply to quantity, size, physical characteristics, composition, the way in which an article was made – handmade when in fact it was mass produced – and its fitness for purpose, etc; the list could be said to be almost limitless.

A breach of the Act is committed if a false description is applied to services provided. Thus, if the owner of a livery stable was foolish enough to advertise or tell potential customers that a groom would be in attendance twenty-four hours a day, when this was not the case, this would be an offence. An offence would also be committed by a riding school which claimed falsely that qualified teachers only were used.

Another important facet of the Act is concerned with pricing. It becomes a criminal offence to say of goods that they are being sold at less than the manufactuer's recommended price if this is not the case. It is also an offence to mark goods or to advertise them at a price less than the trader will accept. This means that if a saddler, for example, advertises or marks tack on a price tag as being £X and then tells potential customers it costs more, an offence is committed. On the other hand, the trader does not have to sell the goods at the price marked as this is only what the law terms an invitation to treat. He may refuse to sell the goods at the price advertised or marked without committing an offence.

Finally, if a trader seeks to reduce or sell off a range of tack which has not sold well, he is committing an offence if he says the price of goods is reduced, or is the same as when the goods were offered on an earlier occasion, when this is untrue. The law states that the previous price, if this is to figure in an advertisement or a price tag, must be one which the seller had charged for a continuous period of twenty-eight days at some time during the previous six months, and eagle-eyed shoppers will have seen such notices to this effect displayed in some stores at annual or half-yearly sales.

The law is not one sided and provides defences for traders, one of which is human error in the marking of prices. Nor is it an offence if a horse dealer does *not* reveal any particular vice or fault about a horse, although the contrary might be the case if a buyer asked if a horse had a particular vice or fault and the dealer, knowing this to be the case, remained silent.

The drawback from the point of view of an animal owner who has bought goods or services which were falsely described is that to take action under the Act a prosecution has to be brought in a magistrates' court, although cases of extreme false descriptions can be sent for trial at a crown court where the penalties which can be imposed are tougher. This may not always help the consumer because although a court has the power to order compensation to be paid by an offender, it does not always do so. So the complainant would still have to look to a civil court for any recovery of money.

Services
One of the drawbacks of the Sale of Goods Act 1979, and its predecessor Act of the same name passed in 1893, was that it applied to goods only and not to services. Although the courts gave remedies to those who had suffered as a result of receiving negligent services, the position remained unsatisfactory from the consumer's point of view until the passing of the Supply of Goods and Services Act 1982 which came into force on 1 January 1983. The Act codified protection available to consumers as far as the provision of services was involved.

It also had another major purpose and that was to protect people who got goods by way of barter, though not in the true old-fashioned sense of the word. The Act gave those people who obtained goods free by way of exchanging saved coupons, etc, issued by manufacturers as part of a sales drive for a certain range of products, the right to receive goods of merchantable quality as they are entitled to if purchasing in the normal manner.

The Act laid down three criteria for services:

They will be carried out with reasonable care and skill;
The work will be done within a reasonable time;
The charge will be reasonable.

The first criterion, although perfectly straightforward on the surface, is worth looking at further to ascertain what is meant by the work being carried out with reasonable care and skill. A farrier who is experienced and qualified by apprenticeship and years or work at the trade should be expected to shoe horses in a perfectly satisfactory manner, as should a tiler be expected to re-roof or repair a stable, and no doubt these factors would be held in the balance should a claim for damages arise as a result of work being carried out without reasonable care and skill.

Doubtless one important yardstick which will be considered is the question of cost. As has been observed elsewhere in this book, courts tend to take a robust view of cost by holding that a person gets what he pays for – and there is much truth in the viewpoint that a cut price may easily equate to a cut-price job.

The next criterion, that the work will be done within a reasonable time, will be a boon to those who have waited an unconscionably long time for repair work to be done. The rider who wants a saddle repaired and the stable owner whose premises need to be put right before winter sets in certainly do not want the work to be started and then left unfinished for weeks because something more profitable has turned up for the workmen. They are entitled to expect that the work will be carried out, if not immediately, then at least without undue delay.

Under the Supply of Goods and Services Act, if a delay in undertaking a job is unreasonable a claim for damages can be sustained. So what is reasonable? It is, perhaps, easier to explain by saying that it is unreasonable for a person seeking a service which takes, say, two days to do the work satisfactorily, to expect it to be done in less than that time. In deciding if the wait for a saddle to be repaired is reasonable or not, it would be necessary to show how long the work should take when carried out by an experienced and skilled craftsman, plus a reasonable time for the work to go through the system.

Finally, the third criterion, that the charge will be reasonable, has to be met. In deciding what is reasonable a court will take into account the number of man hours necessary to carry out the job properly, plus the cost of any replacements required and material used, and a percentage of the total cost as the profit factor. If a price for repairing a saddle was quoted and accepted then this becomes a contract and must be adhered to by those providing the service. It is when no cost is quoted that disputes arise, and under the Act the onus is on the person charging for the service to prove that his charge was reasonable in all the circumstances.

Ring auctions

Horses are frequently sold by auction and sales do not become binding until the auctioneer brings down his hammer and announces that the horse is sold to the person making the final bid. Until that time the bidder is free to withdraw and the auctioneer also free to withdraw the lot, which might well happen if the reserve price has not been reached. The reserve price is not known to those bidding and even if an auctioneer has brought down his hammer by mistake and accepted a bid below the reserve, the seller is still entitled to withdraw the horse.

In practice it is possible for the seller to bid for the horse he has put up for sale in an attempt to push the price up, and this is usually done through an agent. If this course of conduct is to be followed by the seller a notice must be exhibited in the sale catalogue or advertisement. Obviously, sellers do from time to time use the services of an agent to push up prices without revealing this to the public. Any sales effected in this manner are not legally binding and a buyer is entitled to return the horse or other purchase and have his money refunded in full.

Auction 'rings' have been outlawed by the Auctions (Bidding Agreements) Acts of 1927 and 1969. Although they undoubtedly continue to go on, the writer has no evidence that they exist in those auctions where horses come under the hammer.

An auction ring is usually operated by a number of dealers and works in the following manner. A horse of some value known to a number of dealers is offered for sale at an auction. Dealers who would normally be expected to bid against one another for a good horse decide among themselves before the auction that only one will bid, thus ensuring that the price is not forced up and the true price may not be reached. If the horse is knocked down to the participating dealer, it is then auctioned between those dealers not taking part and the balance between the price paid at the auction and the price reached at the subsequent 'ring' auction is split between all those participating.

If the seller of the horse later discovers the existence of the ring he is entitled under Section 3 of the 1969 Act to the return of the horse and may sue any person who was party to the agreement not to bid. Unfortunately, sellers are rarely able to invoke the protection the law offers in this respect through ignorance of a 'ring' operating.

Although conditions of auctions may vary, the usual practice is that a deposit of 10 per cent has to be paid by the buyer to the auctioneer, with the balance to follow within the time specified. In most cases the statutory applied terms as to quality, fitness for purpose, etc. described earlier in this chapter do not apply, so buying at an auction is very much a case of *caveat emptor*.

Mail order

Horses are not sold by mail order but much of the necessary riding clothing and some equipment is and, because there have been fraudulent practices in the past in connection with such transactions, a number of statutory and voluntary regulations and codes of practice have been introduced to protect buyers.

The Mail Order Transactions (Information) Order 1976 lays down that when a buyer is asked to send money in advance, a post office box number is not sufficient to identify the seller. Consequently, all advertisements in which money is asked for in advance must contain the name and full postal address of the business concerned.

The Advertising Standards Authority deals with complaints about advertisements which are not 'legal, decent, honest and truthful'. The Authority insists in its Code of Advertising Practice that all mail order advertisments, except those in catalogues of firms which specialise in mail order business, offer full refund of money when unwanted goods are returned in an undamaged condition within seven days of being received, and calls for a 'money back if not satisfied' declaration or its equivalent.

Most mail order firms stipulate a maximum period for delivery, which is usually twenty-eight days, and a buyer is entitled to endorse any order with the warning that if the goods are not delivered within a certain time – twenty-eight days would be reasonable – the contract is cancelled and money paid must be refunded.

The major mail order companies which sell a vast range of goods through catalogues are members of the Mail Order Traders' Association. This association has its own code of practice, binding on all members, which covers goods not of merchantable quality, goods unfit for their purpose or different from what the buyer ordered and those damaged in transit. Details of the code are to be found in the catalogues.

Most mail order advertisments are to be found in newspapers and magazines and many reputable publications subscribe to a scheme run by their particular publishing association to afford protection to purchasers, which undertakes to refund money paid to firms which subsequently go into liquidation.

3 GRAZING

Land is rented for a horse to be grazed on but later the owner of the land allows a local scrap dealer to store waste material in a corner of the field. As a result the horse is injured.

Who is responsible?

The example quoted above is one of many which the owner of a horse or pony may face at any time and 'horror' stories relating to land leased for grazing are legion. One of the main problems which many animal owners face today is a shortage of suitable grazing land where the horse can live in safety, especially in large urban centres. As a result any owner of land is in a position of being able to demand and get any sum by way of rent which the market will bear at the time, quite often for land which is totally unsafe for a horse to graze.

No one in his right mind would lease a house, flat or shop, without reading and understanding a lease which sets out not only his rights and responsibilities but those of the landlord. Similarly, no one would rent accommodation for any period of time without getting a rent book which, in any event, the law demands. Unfortunately this is not the case when grazing land is rented and, because of its shortage, the average owner is all too often at the mercy of a landowner who can be, and frequently is, quite thoughtless in his dealings.

One of the main difficulties any horse owner is likely to come across when considering legal action for negligence against the owner of rented grazing land on which a horse has been injured is establishing that a legal tenancy in fact exists. The experience of many horse owners has shown that few landowners are prepared to enter into any type of written agreement upon which the owner of an injured horse can sue, so it becomes a matter of argument as to just what contractual arrangement was entered into between landowner and horse owner. Indeed, the landowner may claim that there was never any intention on his part to create a legal relationship.

There may be any number of reasons why such a landowner does not wish to reduce any grazing agreement to writing, some valid and some dubious; one which comes to mind in the latter category is the chance to make extra income by receiving rent in cash which is not declared to the Inland Revenue. Nevertheless, there are reputable landowners who are prepared to enter into written grazing agreements, a specimen of which appears on page 62.

Even if such an agreement is *not* entered into, there are certain standard legal rights which the horse owner, as tenant of the land on which his animal is being grazed, is entitled to rely upon. The first is what is known to the law as quiet enjoyment of the land. All this means is that, in return for payment of rent at the specified time, the landowner allows the horse to graze the land.

Furthermore, quiet enjoyment can be construed as containing within what is rather an elastic definition the right of the horse to graze on the land without being endangered. For example, if a farmer lets a field for grazing purposes in which there is a yew tree, or if the farmer's land adjoining the field contains a yew tree with overhanging branches, it is incumbent on that farmer to lop the tree so that no branch is within reach of the horse. The reason, as many will no doubt know, is that the yew tree's foliage is poisonous to cattle and horses. A farmer would be expected to know this and ensure that any horses grazing on his land are not exposed to danger.

A similar situation exists with a farmer using a chemical spray or insecticide on a field adjoining grazing land which he knows, or should know, is poisonous to horses. As long as the poisonous substance stays on the adjoining field no harm can come to grazing horses.

In some countries where weather conditions are predictable no problem would arise. In Britain, however, where the weather can change within hours and it is possible to have all four seasons within a spell of a week, a wind can suddenly spring up and blow the spray or insecticide on to the field in which horses are grazing.

At first sight many would think that the farmer could not be held responsible for changes in the weather or the direction of the wind. This is so: but a farmer, whose very living can depend on the weather, should be aware of the vagaries of the British climate and realise the potential danger. In such circumstances the farmer may well be guilty of negligence.

Indeed, it could be argued with equal force that even if the horses were grazing in an adjoining field which did not belong to the farmer, the farmer should have been aware of the potential danger and might still be liable in damages for any misfortune. (It may seem that the instance quoted here is far fetched, but this is an actual case known to the author.)

An example was quoted at the beginning of this chapter of a field let for grazing on which the owner subsequently allowed a scrap dealer to deposit waste material. In a true case of this a horse impaled itself on a piece of iron. Fortunately, the injury, although serious, did not prove fatal but inevitably led to the owner of the horse having to pay veterinary fees. Again, this was an instance of the landowner not allowing his tenant – the owner of the horse – quiet enjoyment of the rented grazing land.

So what remedy does the law afford the horse owner whose animal is injured in these circumstances? First of all there is a claim for breach of contract, the contract being the agreement for the horse to be grazed on the land.

There is no doubt that, in the circumstances already described, there was a breach of contract in as much as the landowner did not keep his land in such a condition that it was safe for a horse to graze. By the very nature of such a contract, safety of the horse must be implied, otherwise there would be no point in the owner of the animal paying for grazing rights.

On the other hand, in the absence of a written contract, it could be difficult to prove that this was implied in the contract. The landowner, if of an unscrupulous disposition, could, and probably would, argue that if a verbal contract existed the horse owner knew of potential dangers existing in the field and undertook that risk. In such a case it would be a question of whose word a court accepted.

If, however, the potential danger did not exist at the time of the grazing agreement being entered into but was brought on to the land by the owner at a later date, a claim could lie for breach of contract or in tort, the latter being based on the fact that the landowner should have foreseen the potential danger and was negligent in allowing such a danger on to his land.

In the case of the horse poisoned by eating foliage from overhanging branches of a yew tree growing in an adjoining field, the owner of the land on which the tree was growing would be liable under what is known as the Strict Liability Rule and it would not be necessary to prove either negligence or lack of care.

The rule of law of strict liability was first pronounced in the case of *Rylands* v *Fletcher* (1868) by Mr Justice Blackburn when he declared: '. . . the person who for his own purposes brings on his lands and collects and keeps there anything likely to do mischief if it escapes, must keep it at his peril, and if he does not do so is *prima facie* answerable for all the damage which is the natural consequence of its escape.'

This pronouncement was approved two years later by the House of Lords and although the subject matter of the litigation was a reservoir, the principle was extended in the case of *Crowhurst* v *Burial Board of Amersham* (1878) to cover yew trees. The facts of that case were very simple: the plaintiff was riding his horse alongside the boundary of a cemetery where yew trees grew, and the horse ate the foliage and consequently died. If the horse had eaten the poisonous foliage within the boundaries of the cemetery the rule would not have applied because the foilage would not have 'escaped', although some other cause of action might have been possible. This particular case should serve as a warning to anyone who has yew trees on their land that branches should be cut back so they are out of reach of animals.

The two examples cited are based on injury to horses which were the sole occupants of grazing land. The problem becomes more complicated if the landowner lets land to more than one horse owner, for there are two main points to bear in mind: first, the quality of the grazing itself and second, the horses to be grazed on the land.

As far as the quality of grazing is concerned it has to be remembered that there are two reasons why land is rented for grazing. One is that it is a place where a horse or horses can be kept safely; the second is that, for part of the year at least, the horse can live off the land without the need of the owner to provide fodder. Whether or not any particular piece of grazing land will provide sufficient fodder for more than one horse depends on the size and state of the land, which makes it absolutely essential that the horse owner inspects the land and makes a judgement on these points.

If the person leasing or renting the land is fortunate enough to find a landowner who is prepared to enter into a proper leasing agreement – and some are – that person can ask for a clause to be inserted into the agreement limiting the number of horses to be grazed on the land: whether or not this would result in an increased rent being payable is a matter for discussion between the two parties.

Where horses share grazing land there is always the possibility of one of them having bad habits and being prone to such bad behaviour as kicking or biting the others. In these circumstances it becomes difficult to seek to assess the culpability or otherwise of the landowner if one of the horses is injured.

It would be necessary to prove that the landowner was aware of the vices of the particular horse but chose to ignore them. In such cases the landowner can with truth be said to have acted unreasonably and without foresight for the consequences of permitting a horse with bad habits to share grazing land with other horses, so an action could lie. If the landowner was unaware of the propensity of a horse to savage other equines and had the misfortune to be sued, he could join the owner of that particular horse as a co-defendant in the action and in all probability would be successful in passing the blame on to the owner.

In theory this is fine but in practice it does not always work out because the incident in question might have been the first time a horse exhibited bad habits. Before it is possible to sue the owner of the horse with bad habits it is necessary to prove that the owner *knew* of those habits and did nothing about taking precautions to minimise possible damage (see also Chapter 9).

One danger which frequently arises when grazing is shared by a number of horses is when a colt or entire horse is grazed in a field with a filly or mare which comes into season. Not every owner of a mare wants the additional expense involved in the safe birth of a foal, to say nothing of the expense of extra feeding.

Whether or not it would be possible to sue the landowner for breach of duty of care owed to the owner of the mare would depend on the extent of his knowledge as to when the female was due to come into season. If the mare was in season when the male animal was introduced into the field without prior warning, the landowner could be said to be in breach of his duty of care and if the owner of the mare had sole grazing rights, also in breach of contract.

There is no hard and fast rule or set of principles which can be laid down and on which the horse owner can safely rely as far as injury, or the risk of pregnancy, to an animal is concerned. Each case has to be dealt with on its own merits within the principles of law and within those broad principles one case can succeed while a similar but not identical one will fail.

This is perhaps an appropriate moment to explain what is meant by the principle of the law of torts that imposes on people a general duty of care not to cause injury to another's person or damage to another's goods by carelessness.

Like many instances of principles of law, this did not arise overnight; in fact, it was developed over many years and was really crystallised in its present form in the early years of the last century. Since then, situations where such a general duty of care exists have been identified and incorporated into the law. Interestingly enough, the law in medieval times recognised that farriers who carried out their work in such a way as to cause injury to a horse showed a lack of care of which the law would take note. Not surprising, perhaps, when the importance is realised of the role played by the horse in times of peace and war.

But it was not until 1932 that the great jurist Lord Atkin put forward in general terms his conception of what comprised the duty of care. This was in the case of *Donoghue* v *Stevenson*, which started in Scotland when the appellant claimed damages for the distress she suffered on finding a decomposed snail in a bottle of ginger beer bought for her in a shop.

The case was originally thrown out by the court in Scotland, but in argument before the House of Lords it was generally agreed by lawyers in the case that the laws of both Scotland and England were the same for this purpose: that to support an action in negligence, it was necessary for the plaintiff to show a duty of care was owed to him and that there had been a breach of that duty.

The argument was whether the manufacturer of the ginger beer had a general duty of care to the appellant who was at the end of a chain of events. The manufacturer sold the ginger beer to the shopkeeper who sold it in the normal course of business to the friend who had purchased it for the plaintiff. So was the ultimate consumer too remote from the manufacturer, because of the chain of events, for the manufacturer to owe a general duty of care?

Lord Atkin seized the opportunity to make the law clear in accordance with what he described as sound common sense. The general conception of the duty of care he propounded in his judgment was that reasonable care has to be taken to avoid acts or omissions which can be reasonably foreseen to be likely to injure your neighbour – 'neighbour' being defined as any person or persons so closely affected by another's person's act that that person ought reasonably to bear in mind the probability of a particular act or omission having an affect on someone else.

Lord Atkin's test plays an important role in establishing two main points. The first is that if it is not possible to assume a duty of care, such duty must be established by showing that likelihood of injury was something which ought reasonably to have been foreseen; if this is the case, a duty of care may exist, lack of which can be treated as negligence. One certainty is that if no duty of care exists there can be no negligence.

So it can be seen that the owner of a horse which is injured while grazing as a result of the landowner's positive act, or act of omission, is also likely to have a case, not only for breach of contract but alternatively in tort. And if there is a dispute as to whether or not a contract exists, it is reassuring that there is in tort a second string to the bow of litigation.

So far the examples cited have been in connection with the acts or omissions of landowners, but the law is not a one-way street. Apart from the obligation to pay rent for use of the land, the horse owner may have an obligation to maintain the land, which could even extend to the repair of fences. If this is the case, the owner whose horse strays on to a road and is injured can have no claim against the landowner because the horse owner has been in breach of his obligations. Obviously, if any contract is silent about maintenance of land and/or fences and a horse strays, the landowner would be culpable for any injury which befell a straying horse, not so much in tort, but for breach of contract in failing to ensure that the grazing land was secure for its purpose.

It is, of course, a counsel of perfection to urge all horse and pony owners seeking grazing land to have a formal agreement drawn up, but owners should beware of dealing with people who are not prepared to be bound by such an agreement. In those areas where grazing land is in short supply, it is understandable that the horse owner would be unwilling to antagonise a future landlord by insisting on such an agreement for fear of losing the grazing.

There are precautions which can and should be taken. The earliest method, after the deal has been struck verbally and rent paid in advance, is to write a letter of thanks to the landowner for accommodating the particular horse or pony, incorporating what are understood to be the terms of the agreement. A photocopy of the letter should be kept.

By no stretch of the imagination could this be construed as a written contract but it serves a useful purpose. For the horse owner it sets out what he considers to be the terms and conditions of the agreement. It also puts the landowner on notice that this is what his tenant considers to be part of the deal. If the landlord does not like it or disagrees, he is in a position to raise the matter and from his point of view it is preferable for it to be done in writing.

CONTRACT FOR GRAZING RIGHTS

An agreement dated .... 198 . . between......................
(THE OWNER) (1) and ....
of .... (THE GRAZIER) (2)
WHEREBY IT IS AGREED:

1 The grazier shall be entitled for the period starting ....
.... 198.....and ending .... to graze his/her (3)
horse(s) on the field/land (4).......................................
.... (5) being
part of ....Farm/land at...............................
.... (6)

2 The grazier has paid £...................... to the owner (as he
hereby acknowledges) for the said right or the grazier will pay
the sum of £ ....weekly.

3 The grazier shall keep the field including all fences, gates
and other appurtenances in at least the same condition as it now
is and shall be responsible to maintain all such fences, gates and
appurtenances in such condition to prevent his horse(s) (4)
straying or being injured.

4 The grazier warrants that the horse(s) (4) is/are (4) not
vicious, unruly, destructive or diseased.

5 The grazier shall be liable for any loss or damage caused by
the horse(s) (4) or any of them (4) either by straying or
otherwise.

6 The owner shall not do or cause to be done or put in the field
anything which shall cause injury or other damage to the
horse(s) (4) or any of them (4) and shall compensate the grazier
in respect of any loss resulting therefrom.

7 The owner shall be entitled by notice in writing to terminate
this agreement forthwith on the death of the grazier or any
breach by the grazier of the terms of this agreement. AS
WITNESS the hands of the parties on the date hereinbefore
mentioned.

Signed by the Owner..............(1) in the presence of.........(7)
Signed by the Grazier ....(2) in the presence of.........(7)

Notes:
(1) Name of owner.
(2) Name of grazier.
(3) Specify the number of horses to be grazed.
(4) Delete as appropriate.
(5) Insert sufficient description adequate to identify the field/land; eg the two acre field
    Ordnance survey number .... on the
    Ordnance Survey (..................... edition).
(6) Insert postal address of farm or land of which the field forms part.
(7) Witness should sign and insert his/her address and occupation.

General: This agreement should be signed by both parties in duplicate so both have a copy for future reference.

This is a straightforward agreement and, indeed, nothing more complicated is really required. It begins by naming the parties to the agreement and specifying for how long the agreement shall last. Normally, it will run for a year, thus giving both sides a clear-cut understanding of the duration of the agreement.

It is essential that the horse owner should have a firm indication of how long grazing will be required and this should be taken into account when deciding the length of the agreement. A similar consideration should be in the mind of the landowner. If, as far as the grazier is concerned, there is an element of uncertainty as to how long grazing will be required, the following, eighth, point can be added:

8   The grazier shall be entitled by notice in writing to terminate this agreement within four weeks of said notice being delivered.

It will be seen that this is creating limits of time for the life of the agreement which can only be beneficial to both sides, and at the same time it states unequivocally what the rental shall be for the life of the agreement.

There is nothing particularly harsh about condition three, which lays on the grazier the responsibility of keeping the land, fences, etc, in at least the same condition that it was in at the time of the agreement. This is a normal clause and is not unlike the undertaking given by tenants of houses, flats, shops and other property that they will be responsible for certain aspects of maintenance.

Clause four is important as the landowner is entitled to know whether or not a particular horse has any bad traits and, if other animals are to be grazed as well, whether it is free from disease likely to infect other livestock.

Although clause five may seem to be onerous, as it places responsibility for damage done by straying horses on the grazier rather than the landowner, it is in keeping with the clause requiring the grazier to maintain fences. Graziers must use their common sense and decide whether or not they wish to have this clause included, and would obviously take into account the condition of fences, gates, etc, at the time of entering into such an agreement.

Clause six places responsibility fairly and squarely on the landowner to maintain the field in a safe condition. This would cover any rubbish being dumped on the land and even the introduction of a horse of a vicious nature. It is arguable that such a clause would, if the landowner was a farmer and adjoining fields were used for agricultural purposes, cover the circumstance referred to earlier where a poisonous spray was carried on to the grazing land through the farmer's lack of care or foresight.

The specimen agreement does have one drawback: it does not specifically cater for the situation, which is quite common, where more than one owner grazes a horse on the same land. From the point of view of the landowner this creates no problem because all that is necessary is to amend clause three to read: 'The grazier(s) shall jointly and severally . . .'. The insertion of this phrase will protect the landowner as it gives him the right to proceed, if such a step is necessary, against one or all of those who graze horses. Consequently this puts each individual horse owner in a vulnerable position as he may be held responsible for the omissions of others, and must depend on the good sense and willingness of his fellow graziers to co-operate in maintaining fences, etc.

The answer in these circumstances is for all horse owners to reduce to writing any agreement they come to as to how the physical work involved in maintaining the field, fences and appurtenances is to be apportioned. Alternatively, they must decide how much each individual member is to be responsible to the others for any financial recompense that may have to be paid if there is a failure to carry out maintenance.

Unfortunately it is not a practical proposition to give an example of such an agreement here because each will certainly have slightly different features which are relevant only to the particular grazing rights. Nevertheless, it is not beyond the capabilities of anyone blessed with average intelligence and common sense to draft a joint agreement, although it must be stressed that good will is called for on the part of all concerned.

4 STABLES AND LIVERY

What rights does an owner have when in exchange for free livery in a riding establishment the horse is used for giving riding lessons?

Placing a horse at a livery stable

As more and more people take up riding and the horse population increases, the shortage of stabling and grazing is likely to become more acute. Apart from a comparatively few fortunate owners who have their own facilities, most have to place their horses at livery or in riding schools. Normally this will be a straightforward transaction, provided the weekly or monthly bills can be met, but the wise owner will satisfy himself that the establishment is not only run by qualified people but also carries insurance which covers animals stabled in the quarters.

It is also important to establish just what services are to be provided. These can cover exercising the horse, shoeing (in some establishments), or owner's use of a covered school or menage for so many hours a week, etc. Obviously, feeding the horse should be part and parcel of any contractual agreement entered into, as should proper exercise and shoeing of a horse, but what happens if the animal falls ill or meets with an injury while on the premises and needs veterinary attention?

Common sense dictates that the stable staff, who probably see much more of the horse than the owner, should be alert and watch for the first signs of any illness or condition which will require specialist attention. From the point of view of the livery stable owner, it is essential that any stabling agreement should include a condition giving the establishment the right to call in a veterinary surgeon and to be indemnified, as far as fees are concerned, by the owner of the horse. An experienced stable owner will be able to tell whether or not veterinary advice is needed and the law would expect him to act in a reasonable manner in this respect. Obviously the owner of the livery should have the right of insisting that a horse which develops an infectious disease must be removed; otherwise he could be held liable if other horses were infected.

Unfortunately there are a number of people who expect livery fees to cover veterinary fees as well and inevitably this leads to disputes, although the law might well presume that the stable owner was acting as agent for the horse owner when

68

calling in a veterinary surgeon and was entitled to be indemnified.

Questions to ask

Riding stables are not charitable institutions. They are businesses and can be expected to conduct the business in order to maximise profits. In some areas, livery fees may be too high for the owner of a horse or pony seeking accommodation for his animal. In cases such as these it is becoming more and more common for the owner of an animal to enter into an arrangement by which livery fees are either waived entirely or reduced in return for the stable having the use of the horse for its own purposes, usually to hire out to riders or for use as part of a riding school.

On the surface this is an excellent scheme; the owner stables his horse either free of charge or at a reduced rate, the animal is assured of exercise and the owner of the stable makes money out of the horse. Beneath the surface, however, is a veritable minefield, as many owners have discovered as far as the health and condition of their horses are concerned. Unless strict conditions are agreed as to who may ride the animal and how often it should be used during any given period of time, it is possible that the horse could be overworked or injured if ridden by an indifferent rider.

The horse owner should ask the following questions:

How many hours a day or week will my horse be worked?
Who will ride the horse and will he/she be questioned as to their capability to ride the animal?
If used for riding lessons, will care be taken to see that the horse is used properly?

Many more questions could be asked but all concern the welfare of the horse and much will depend, in the case of a riding school offering working livery, on the arrangements finally arrived at between owner and school.

There is probably no form of livery more likely to lead to disputes than this type unless both sides are absolutely certain what form of work the horse will undertake. Owners must remember that if it is decided that from Monday to Friday their horses shall be at the disposal of the riding stable, it is no good turning up during that period and demanding use of the horses. Obviously, if no rides or lessons have been booked at the particular time, the owner of the stable probably will have no objections to owners taking out their own horses but he would not, in law, be bound to allow them to do so. Consequently, before entering into any agreement of this type, horse owners should insist on a written contract outlining all important details.

DIY livery

Grass livery has already been discussed at length but there is one other form which is becoming popular – the Do-It-Yourself livery, which strictly speaking is not really livery. DIY livery involves an owner renting stabling either with or without grazing and undertaking all the work of looking after the horse. Although this is an economic method of obtaining livery there are obvious disadvantages, the main one being that the owner has to be available for looking after the horse in all ways and probably, apart from basic security of the stables, cannot expect the owner of the stables to take much responsibility for the particular horse.

Insurance and contracts

Whatever sort of livery is used, if it is one which involves accommodation on commercially-run premises owners of horses should in their own interests establish whether or not the owner of the stables carries insurance to cover death or injury, or even theft of a horse. Although the requirements of the Riding Establishments Act 1964 stipulates that there must be insurance against liability for injury to other persons, there is nothing in the legislation to cover the other risks mentioned. The sensible horse or pony owner will, therefore, take his or her own steps as far as insurance of an animal is concerned.

The various types of livery discussed here all involve the horse owner entering into a contractual relationship with the livery stable proprietor. Any breaches of the conditions of such agreements or injury to horses as a result of the negligence of the proprietor and/or his employees becomes a breach of contract for which the law will provide a remedy. Obviously, owners of livery must protect themselves and it surely would not be unreasonable for them to insist, as part of the contract, that a horse which becomes unruly or extremely difficult to handle should be removed by the owner.

If the horse owner wishes to avail himself of a legal remedy his case will be stronger if he has a written agreement with the proprietor of the stable. This, it is readily admitted, is a counsel of perfection, and much easier to suggest than to carry out.

If the subject of a written agreement is raised by a horse owner in respect of all livery arrangements, apart from full or grass, and for any reason the proprietor of the stable fails to deliver such an agreement, there is one precaution the horse owner can take. This is to write to the proprietor setting out all the conditions attached to the agreement as far as the horse owner understands, with a concluding sentence on the following lines: 'Unless I hear to the contrary from you within fourteen days that my understanding is wrong, I shall take it that you agree with these terms.'

Such a letter would not constitute a binding contract but as, in law, a verbal contract is as binding as a written one, such a letter would strengthen a horse owner's case as a judge would be likely to hold that it gave the stable proprietor an opportunity to challenge the understood terms. Although the law requires a positive agreement between contracting parties and silence on the part of one of the parties cannot really be said to imply agreement, it can be persuasive.

Strictly speaking, an oral agreement as to terms later recorded in writing could well be said to be not a written contract but a verbal agreement evidenced in writing. The importance of seeking to have any agreement reduced in writing, and with both parties being perfectly certain that that was what they intended, is twofold. As stated previously, while a verbal contract can be just as binding it is far more open to

71

question as to what both parties intended and ultimately a judge has to decide in favour of one person or the other: this may well be the person not only with the better memory but also a better demeanour and performance in the witness box if a conflict should ever come to court.

Building your own stables

There are some horse and pony owners who are fortunate to live on a farm where livery is no problem, and many others – mostly in the country – whose homes have sufficient space for stables to be built on their own land.

The old adage that an Englishman's home is his castle is not always applicable these days, especially as far as planning laws and requirements are concerned. In many respects local planning requirements restrict home owners from making radical and far-reaching changes without consent, but there are concessions and these can be applied to the erection of stables, coach house, etc, within the curtilage of a dwelling house.

There is nothing significant about 'curtilage': it is a word of antiquity which is defined as an area attached to a dwelling house as part of its enclosure. In most cases this would be taken to mean a garden but it could also include a paddock or orchard which forms part of the grounds of a dwelling house.

A person who wishes to enlarge, improve or otherwise alter a dwelling house is regarded as a 'permitted developer' and as such has no need to seek planning permission from the local planning authority as long as certain limits are observed, which at the time of writing are:

1(a) The cubic content of the original dwelling house (as ascertained by its external measurements) is not exceeded by more than (i) in the case of a terrace house, 50 cubic metres or 10 per cent or whichever is the greater or (ii) in any other case, 70 cubic metres or 15 per cent whichever is the greater, subject in both cases to a maximum of 115 cubic metres;

(b) The height of the building as so enlarged, improved or altered, does not exceed the height of the highest part of the roof of the original dwelling house;

72

(c) No part of the building as so enlarged, improved or altered, projects beyond the forwardmost part of any wall of the original dwelling house which fronts on a highway;

(d) No part of the building as so enlarged, improved or altered, which lies within a distance of two metres from any boundary of the curtilage of the dwelling house has, as a result of the development, a height exceeding four metres.

2(a) The area of ground covered by buildings within the curtilage (other than the original dwelling house) does not thereby exceed 50 per cent of the total area of the curtilage excluding the ground area of the original dwelling house:

Provided that:

(a) The erection of a garage or coach house within the curtilage of the dwelling house shall be treated as the enlargement of the dwelling house for all purposes of this permission (including the calculation of cubic content) if any part of that building lies within a distance of five metres from any part of the dwelling house;

(b) The erection of a stable or loose box anywhere within the curtilage of the dwelling house shall be treated as the enlargement of the dwelling house for all purposes of this permission (including the calculation of cubic content);

(c) For the purpose of this permission the extent to which the cubic content of the original dwelling house is exceeded shall be ascertained by deducting the amount of the cubic content of the dwelling house as enlarged, improved or altered (whether such enlargement, improvement or alteration was carried out in pursuance of this permission or otherwise);

(d) Where any part of the dwelling house will, as a result of the development, lie within a distance of five metres from an existing garage or coach house, that building shall for the purpose of the calculation of the cubic content, be treated as forming part of the dwelling house as enlarged, improved or altered; and,

(e) The limitation contained in sub-paragraph (d) above shall not apply to development consisting of (i) the insertion of a window, including a dormer window, into a wall or the roof of the original dwelling house, or the alteration or enlargement of an existing window or (ii) any other alterations to any part of the roof of the original dwelling house.

3 A check should be made that there is no Article 4 Direction in force on the area. If so, it means that planning permission is

required for any building or installation.

4   Attention is also drawn to the following points:

(a) Building Regulations as opposed to planning requirements, may be applicable and checks should be made as to whether or not plans and materials to be used in the construction need approval;

(b) In National Parks, areas of outstanding natural beauty and conservation areas, the limits on the permitted extension of a dwelling house remain at 50 cubic metres or 10 per cent whichever is the greater with the maximum remaining at 115 cubic metres;

Where a dwelling house has already been extended up to the permitted limits (whether by its present or former occupier) planning permission will be required for any further extension. This applies wherever the dwelling house is situated;

(c) Where a dwelling house has already been extended up to the permitted limits (whether by its present or former occupier) planning permission will be required for any further extension;

(d) Approval under the Building Regulations and the granting of planning permission are two separate procedures and the gaining of approval of plans and materials does not necessarily mean that planning permission will be granted in cases where it is required;

(e) The erection of a garage or coach house in the areas cited in (b) above counts as enlargement of the dwelling house anywhere within the curtilage. A stable or loose box always counts as an enlargement of the dwelling house.

Although at first sight these concessions may appear to be couched in archaic and legalistic terms they are, in fact, the model of clarity as far as some regulations are concerned. The main thing for anyone to bear in mind when thinking of building a stable in the grounds of their home is the need for accuracy with a tape measure in ascertaining whether or not the stable comes within the permitted development without planning permission.

It is interesting to note that, under 2(b) above, a stable or loose box, which is almost certainly to be built as a separate structure away from the main dwelling house, is seen as an enlargement of the house rather than as a separate building.

There are two further points which must be noted and considered by anyone wishing to build a stable or loose box within the boundary of their home. The first concerns building regulations which deals with precise standards of construction, safe design and choice of materials to be used, as opposed to planning which concerns the way land is developed and the effect of proposed development on its surroundings as well as environmental and preservation issues. So it is possible that even where planning permission has been granted, a building can fall foul of the various building regulations which are the responsibility of the local district council, which may also be the planning authority.

If permission for a block of stables is granted, almost certainly such permission will take into account the building regulations and specify the materials to be used. If permission is not needed, which is most likely to be the case for a single stable or loose box, then it is essential that the materials and form of construction satisfy the building regulations.

An application has to be made in duplicate to the local council whose building inspector will inspect the plans and, possibly, the site. As a result of his report the application may be approved without alteration as far as plans or materials are concerned, or improvements may be suggested. Obviously the plans stand a better chance of being accepted if they are prepared by a reputable local builder or surveyor who will know just what is and, more important, is not, permitted.

It will be necessary also for periodic notices to be given to the local authority so that the various stages of work can be inspected to ensure plans have been adhered to and specified materials for construction used. In the case of a stable, if any damp course, foundation or excavation is to be covered, or concrete or other material is to be used to cover a site of a drain, it is essential that at least twenty-four hours notice of this intention is given to the local authority. If this is not done the building inspector can order the work to be opened up, which is a costly process.

Under the law a person who submits plans and specifications required under the building regulations is entitled to receive a decision within five weeks. Work can commence if nothing has been heard by the end of that time, although it can still be halted if it fails to meet the specifications.

If the plans are complicated – unlikely in the case of a simple stable or loose box – the authority can ask for a further two months to consider them. If the plans and specifications are in any way faulty and the proposed developer refuses the request for an extension of time, the authority has the power to immediately refuse permission and ask the applicant to re-apply: so it really is not worth it to withhold permission. There is a right of appeal against refusal to the local magistrates' court and in some cases to the Department of the Environment.

Many people are tempted to go ahead and carry out building work, in those instances where planning permission is not required, without seeking approval under the building regulations. This is a short-sighted policy for if by chance there is a breach of the regulations, not only is it an offence for which a fine can be imposed, with an additional fine for each day the building stands after conviction, but the local authority can order the building to be pulled down and rebuilt at the owner's expense.

Similarly, if planning permission is required, which is likely to be the case for a stable block rather than an individual stable, or if there is an Article 4 Direction in force and work is done without permission, the offender faces prosecution and a fine on conviction plus the almost inevitable order to pull down the building at his own expense.

The prudent person wishing to build a stable or loose box within the grounds of his residence should check with his local planning authority to see if planning permission is required. It should be possible to get this information by making one telephone call or writing a letter of inquiry.

There is one other factor to take into account whenever a stable, or any addition come to that, has been made and that is insurance. It is highly unlikely that the addition will be included in a blanket household insurance policy and it is essential that any stable should receive the financial protection insurance offers. In the particular equine insurance policy does not cover the horse while in its owner's stable, additional cover should be taken out.

5 VETERINARY AND OTHER SERVICES

A veterinary surgeon prescribes the wrong medication for an ailing horse with the result that the horse becomes seriously ill.

A farrier in shoeing a horse causes injury to a hoof.

What legal remedy does the owner have?

From time to time the services of a veterinary surgeon will be required for any horse or pony; more frequently required will be the services of a farrier, for it is essential that any horse is shod correctly. Unfortunately, mistakes can be made by surgeon or farrier, sometimes with disastrous consequences as far as the animal is concerned, to say nothing of the expense incurred on the part of the owner.

It is a proud boast of English law that it will not allow a wrong to be suffered without providing a remedy. In the circumstances outlined above, the aggrieved owner will seek his remedy in damages and such a claim would be based on breach of contract.

When a horse owner engages the services of a vet, a contract is entered into and it is an implied term of such a contract that the vet will perform his side of the deal in a proper and competent manner, exercising his knowledge and skill to the best of his ability. Because he is a highly-trained professional he knows that owners placing animals in his care are doing so in the expectation that such care will be of a proper standard. The same applies to a blacksmith: the owner of a horse is entitled to expect that the farrier will use his care and skill when shoeing an animal and any act of negligence which causes injury to the animal is actionable.

The failure to exercise these standards of skill and care to which the horse owner is entitled lays the foundation for any claim for damages for breach of contract due to negligence. Nevertheless, each case will depend on its own circumstances and a number of examples will be dealt with.

For instance, although it is important to have a horse inspected by a veterinary surgeon before purchase, this does not mean that the vet can be blamed for negligence if the animal is subsequently found to have a serious or crippling disease. All a veterinary surgeon can do is to give the horse a general examination which will usually reveal its physical condition. If he suspects that the animal may have – or be incubating – some disease he should carry out whatever tests are necessary to establish with a degree of certainty if the horse is unhealthy.

On the other hand there are some equine diseases which cannot be detected until the disease manifests itself or, in extreme cases, will only be established with the aid of a post-mortem. In such cases it would be outrageously unfair to hold the veterinary surgeon liable for negligence in not spotting such a disease or condition at the time of his inspection, and uphold such a charge.

If, however, the veterinary surgeon failed to detect a serious condition which he should have noticed in the course of an examination, then it is reasonable to assume that he did not devote the necessary care to his task which the owner of the horse was entitled to expect and was therefore negligent. In such a case the horse owner is entitled to look to the veterinary surgeon for monetary compensation. Such compensation would take into account a number of factors.

One would be the cost of any medication or specialist treatment needed to cure the horse. If the animal died as a result of the disease, the owner would be entitled to claim from the veterinary surgeon the money thrown away on the purchase of a horse which would not have been bought if the disease had been spotted.

Then there is the problem which crops up from time to time of a mare which is purchased and found later to be in foal. Although it can be argued that the buyer has, as it were, received two horses for the price of one, this can be a mixed blessing. Not only does the new owner incur extra costs in providing a special diet for the mother and her foal, and calling in a veterinary surgeon for the confinement, but there is the consequential problem of finding accommodation and/or grazing for the foal before it can be sold.

Obviously, if the mare was far gone in her pregnancy a competent veterinary surgeon should have recognised her condition. But if the mare was inspected very soon after conception, and there was no reason to suppose the animal had had the opportunity to conceive, there would have been no reason for the vet to suspect the possibility of pregnancy.

The touchstone in such a situation is this: should a veterinary

H&TL—F

surgeon, exercising reasonable skill and judgement in examining the horse, have discovered either a pregnancy or a serious condition? This is a matter for a judge to decide on the balance of probabilities and, no doubt, with the aid of expert witnesses. If the answer to the equation is yes, then the veterinary surgeon was not exercising such a reasonable standard of skill and judgement and was subsequently negligent; if the answer is no, then there was no negligence.

One problem likely to be faced more often by the owner of a riding school or a livery stable than by a private owner is whether or not there is a contractual relationship between the establishment and a veterinary surgeon. For example, if a riding school pays a local veterinary surgeon a retainer to be readily available and he fails to turn out in an emergency, is there a breach of contract and if, as a result, a horse suffers, is the veterinary surgeon negligent?

There can be no doubt that in such circumstances a court would hold the veterinary surgeon to be guilty of negligence if he failed to turn out. And if, as a result of the failure to respond to the call, the owner of the sick or injured animal suffered loss, a claim for damages would lie.

Having said that, it is necessary to qualify the above statement because the veterinary surgeon would have a defence if he could persuade a judge that his action, or lack of action, in not turning out, was reasonable. To establish such a defence the veterinary surgeon would have to show that the owner of the riding school or livery stable had called him out *unreasonably* on previous occasions, when there was no real emergency, and that he had no reason to suppose that this occasion was different. In such a situation, if the veterinary surgeon must have reasonably foreseen the likelihood of this happening there may be negligence, but it is also necessary to establish whether or not a contract exists between the surgeon and the horse owner.

Whenever an animal owner consults a veterinary surgeon there can be no doubt that both are entering into a contractual relationship. In return for veterinary services, although it is most unlikely that before treatment is given there would be any discussion of the cost, the animal owner tacitly implies that the veterinary fees will be met, thus completing the necessary elements for a contractual relationship to be established.

Many vets today insist on being paid at the end of each consultation or treatment, while some are willing to wait for payment until the end of a course of treatment. Whatever the method, undoubtedly, as long as a veterinary surgeon is treating a horse for a specific ailment or injury, a contractual situation exists between the surgeon and the owner. This will continue until either the surgeon gives notice that he will no longer treat the animal or the owner states that he no longer wants the animal treated by that particular person.

It really matters very little that a bill for professional fees may not have been presented, the contract will still exist. Consequently, the refusal of a veterinary surgeon to go out on call to the horse would, it is submitted, be a breach of contract for which damages could be recovered.

It must be stressed that, in the view of the writer, this would apply only to an unanswered call in respect of the condition or injury for which the animal was already being treated. If, during one course of treatment, the horse requires treatment for another, completely unrelated condition, it is arguable that an unanswered call in respect of the new condition would not be held to be negligent. In the absence of a retainer, no contractual relationship as far as that particular condition is concerned exists between veterinary surgeon and owner, although it might be negligent not to point out the new problem.

There is what might be called 'pure' negligence, which can range from making a wrong diagnosis to giving wrong medication to a horse or negligently carrying out a surgical procedure. In such cases it is only necessary to establish wrong treatment to succeed in a claim for damages, although it would also be necessary to prove that such an error was more than just one of judgement.

It is not without profit to look at this stage at the Guide to Professional Conduct, issued by the Royal College of Veterinary Surgeons, which sets out the responsibilities of veterinary surgeons engaged in providing a direct service to the public in relation to the treatment of their animals.

A veterinarian must, say the guidelines, 'make proper provision at all times for the relief of pain and suffering of those animals and for their further treatment, when necessary, either by himself or through professional colleagues . . . once a veterinarian has undertaken a case he should not abandon it without good reason and without safeguarding the welfare of the patient'.

The guidelines also impose the obligation on practitioners that, where professional services cannot be provided in any practice, single-handed or not, at night, weekends or other off-duty periods or due to sickness, holidays or emergencies of any kind, arrangements must be made with colleagues for cover to be provided during the period of absence. The College points out that it is not incumbent upon the sole veterinary practitioner to be on duty twenty-four hours a day, seven days a week, but he must ensure that, when he is off, his clients can obtain professional advice from another veterinarian with whom the practitioner has made prior arrangements.

Breaches of the guidelines would constitute professional misconduct and it is interesting to speculate whether or not a court would find negligence in the legal sense if a practitioner failed to respond to an emergency call or did not provide emergency cover in his absence. To hold that this might be the case would be imposing a great burden on a practitioner. Nevertheless, in certain circumstances, breach of professional ethics could also constitute negligence in the legal sense and a clever barrister who chose to argue this fact could well find the guidelines a persuasive weapon in his armoury.

Obviously a veterinary surgeon is not bound by his code of professional conduct to accept any person as a client, except in an emergency, when he must meet certain obligations, or in an area where he is the only source of advice.

As far as emergency cases are concerned, the Guide to Professional Conduct lays down that any veterinarian, whether he is in a private or salaried capacity, and who is providing a direct service to the public, must make proper provision at all times for the relief of pain and suffering of animals and for their further treatment, when necessary, either by undertaking such treatment himself or through professional colleagues.

Consequently a veterinarian could just not refuse to attend to emergency cases without making alternative arrangements for the treatment of the animal in question. It is of interest that the Appendix to the Guide to Professional Conduct makes the point that a practitioner with a small animal practice, which is most likely to be in an urban area, may be called to help at an accident involving a horse. Obviously, as with doctors, there is specialisation within veterinary medicine and a vet with a small animal practice may not have specialist knowledge of horses. Nevertheless, the small animal practitioner who has been contacted in an emergency involving a horse is under a duty to obtain help from another professional colleague, but remains responsible for the animal until that help arrives.

This raises a point on which it is possible to express an opinion with a good degree of certitude. If a 'small animal veterinarian' attends an injured horse – a species he is unaccustomed to treating – and fails to seek help, there is no doubt that if anything went wrong he would be held to be negligent.

The same principles apply to a farrier as to a veterinary surgeon: if in undertaking the shoeing of a horse he negligently performs the task, causing injury, he is liable. All farrier's are required to serve a four-year apprenticeship and to pass an examination for the diploma of the Worshipful Company of Farriers. Consequently, possession of such a diploma would equate with high standards of care and skill and if a farrier is negligent, there is no reason why he, too, could not be sued. The wise owner will use a farrier with the diploma and should not seek to get a cut-price job. Indeed, it is arguable that a cut price would be equated with a less than adequate job which might be offered by people describing themselves as farrier's but who are not properly qualified.

There is little good, in such cases, in looking to the court for protection should something go wrong and *if* the so-called farrier can be found. Any judge will most likely take a robust view and say that a cut price should, in all the circumstances, have indicated a person not properly qualified to hold himself out as a farrier. Thus the duty of care, which a skilled farrier would owe to his client, would not be so high and, in effect, in seeking a cut-price service the horse owner should have reasonably foreseen the possibility, if not the probability, of getting an inferior job carried out.

Damages, if awarded, would most likely be tailored to take into account this factor. Although the Supply of Goods and Services Act 1982 lays down that a customer is entitled to expect the type of service offered by a farrier to be carried out with reasonable care and skill, the principle outlined above could still apply.

There is one other way in which even a skilled farrier could cause injury to a horse and be liable to damages for so doing. This is if the farrier recommends the use of certain plates which are completely unsuitable for the animal or the task it is going to perform, with unfortunate consequences.

In these circumstances the owner is entitled to look to the farrier for recompense for any loss or damage on the grounds that he was relying on the experience and skill of the farrier to recommend and fit the right plates. A successful claim will depend on proof that the farrier was aware of his client's faith in his abilities. This is not a difficult element to prove. All that is necessary is for the owner to make it perfectly clear to the farrier that he *is* relying on his skill and experience to recommend and fit the right type of plates; it is essential that the farrier is fully aware of the reason why particular plates should be fitted. In fact all owners should take a little time to explain the situation to the farrier when having their animals shod; it could be well worth while.

6 RIDING ACCIDENTS

While taking part in an equestrian event a horse
knocks down and injures a spectator.

Where does the blame lie?

Bearing in mind that the law does not suffer a civil wrong to be done by one person to another without providing a remedy, it is now necessary to look at the rights and responsibilities owed by those who ride horses to each other and to the public in general, as well as the protection riders are entitled to expect from the law.

It would not be an exaggeration to say that the law in this country does not say what we can lawfully do; rather, it prescribes that behaviour which it considers to be anti-social and in most cases linked with the intention to have acted in that way, and stigmatises such behaviour to be criminal and punishable with penal sanctions.

Then there is lawful behaviour which is carried out in such a way as to cause harm to another person and for which recompense is by an award of damages. This type of behaviour which results in an injury or death to a person, or damage to property, is an essential part of the law of tort. A tort is simply an injury to another person and in general terms, as far as this book is concerned, can be summarised as the carrying out of a lawful act in a reckless or negligent manner which causes harm to a third party.

There is no doubt that a horse is an animal which can, in certain circumstances, inflict injury or damage if ridden in a negligent or reckless manner – 'reckless' in the legal sense meaning either a lack of consideration in dealing with others or the intentional creation of unjustifiable risks. Thus reckless riding of a horse can be both a criminal offence and a breach of civil law if injury or damage results, but for the purpose of this chapter only reckless riding as far as the civil law is concerned will be dealt with.

In effect the law says, albeit in a negative manner by its silence, that any person is entitled to ride a horse or pony unless it is in a place where riding is specifically forbidden and providing the animal is ridden in such a way that no harm befalls other people. The reverse is that a person is entitled to expect that while out riding he will be permitted to do so without injury or damage being caused to him or his mount.

In any action for damages in which negligence is alleged as the cause of injury, the burden of proof falls on the plaintiff who has to show that the defendant was, on the balance of probabilities, negligent.

Having said that, it must be admitted that there are exceptions to the necessity of proving negligence under a principle of evidence known as *res ipsa loquitur* – 'the thing speaks for itself'. This rule allows a plaintiff to, in effect, say to a court: 'These are the facts of the accident and unless there was negligence the accident wouldn't have happened.' One example would be if a bale of hay fell from a hayloft on to horse and rider causing the horse to rear up and dislodge its rider who sustained injury. Although the rider knows *what* happened he is unable to say *how* it happened but because of the circumstances, he claims that there had to be negligence. For this principle to be successful in court it would be necessary to show that the falling bale of hay was under the control of the person sued or, if a firm, of its employees, and this would not be difficult.

There is also a defence to an action for negligence known as *volenti non fit injuria*, which can best be translated into everyday terms as follows: if a person consents to the risk of injury he cannot complain if he is, in fact, injured. So if a person who is no more than a moderate rider hires a high-spirited horse from a livery stable, having been warned that the animal is difficult to handle, he cannot later sue the proprietor of the stable for negligence in letting him take out that particular animal.

This doctrine has been applied to injury caused at a gymkhana or show-jumping event although the judicial decisions have, in the view of some academic writers, tended to restrict the principle in general terms. In *Wooldridge* v *Sumner* (1963) the plaintiff, who was a professional photographer, was standing inside a show-jumping arena when a horse ridden by the defendant ran at speed from the course and injured him.

Although the plaintiff was successful in the first instance, the decision was reversed in favour of the defendant by the Court of Appeal where it was held that the ordinary duty of care we all owe to others was not breached by the defendant. The reasoning behind the judgement was that an error of judgement by a sportsman, who was concentrating on the particular event and doing his best to win, did not amount to a breach of duty of care whether the injured person was a spectator, as in effect the plaintiff was, or another participant in the particular event. According to Lord Justice Diplock, as he was then, the decision in favour of the rider was based not on the principle of *volenti non fit injuria* but on the fact that those present were held to have accepted the risk which went with the particular event.

The court held that negligence on the part of the rider was not established. The excessive speed of the horse at the particular corner where the accident occurred was the result of an error of judgement and not negligence. The finding of the trial judge that the horse would have gone on to a cinder track had the rider allowed it to, therefore causing no harm to the plaintiff, was an unjustified inference from the primary facts of the case and, in any event, an attempt to control the horse did not amount to negligence.

In his judgment, which may be seen as of tremendous importance not only to those who take part in show jumping and other equestrian events but also to competitors in any sporting activities with an element of risk to other participants and spectators, Lord Justice Diplock said:

> If, in the course of a game or competition, at a moment when he has not had time to think, a participant by mistake takes a wrong measure he is not to be held guilty of any negligence. . . . A person attending a game or competition takes the risk of any damage caused to him by any act of a participant done in the course of and for the purpose of the game or competition, notwithstanding that such act may involve an error of judgement or a lapse of skill, unless the participant's conduct is such as to evince a reckless disregard of the spectator's safety.

It will be noted that in this remark Lord Justice Diplock was not giving the go-ahead to riders to be negligent without fear of the consequences. He was saying that an error of judgement was not to be looked upon as negligence but that reckless disregard for the safety of spectators would still be actionable.

Nine years later and again in the Court of Appeal, another case involving injury to spectators was heard in which the views of Lord Justice Diplock were reinforced. This case – *Wilks* v *Cheltenham Home Guard Motor Cycle and Light Car Club* – followed the injury of two spectators at a motor cycle scramble when a machine left the course and broke through a roped-off enclosure. The rider was held by the Court of Appeal not to be guilty of negligence. The court held that at an event of that type it was to be expected that loss of control could occur.

The court also held that a competitor (and this would apply with equal force to those taking part in equestrian events) must use reasonable care, having regard to the fact that he was expected to go all out to win and as fast as possible providing he was not foolhardy. It is interesting that the word 'reckless' could have been used equally as well without altering the gravamen of the judgment.

It can be seen that, provided there is no recklessness or foolhardiness, competitors are unlikely to be penalised in damages for injuries caused to spectators at equestrian events even if such injuries are caused by an error of judgement.

There can be no doubt that horses in the hands of inexperienced riders can cause accidents which may result in injury and even the death of a third party, to say nothing of damage to property. In those cases there is only one real point at issue: was the rider negligent?

There is no definite answer to that question because much will depend on the individual circumstances of each case, and negligence can take many forms. Indeed, what might be negligent riding in a busy thoroughfare might not be in a field or on a heath. Furthermore, much would depend on the ability and experience of the individual rider.

The instance of a rider taking out a horse which needs skill and expertise beyond his capabilities has already been referred to as far as the owner of a riding establishment is concerned. But what of the rider of limited ability who takes out a horse which he knows he is really incapable of controlling and meets with an accident? His riding may not constitute negligence in the accepted sense of the word, but sheer incompetence. On the other hand, owing a duty of care to his neighbours, such a rider must be guilty of negligence in the event of an accident in a public place if he was reckless or foolhardy in his choice of a difficult mount.

But, as all riders know, there are circumstances outside their control which can lead to an accident. For instance, a dog may run into the road and bark at a horse, causing it to take fright with disastrous consequences. Is the rider to blame and is there a defence to an action for damages in such a case?

The Animals Act 1971 imposes on owners and those who have control of animals a duty to take reasonable care to prevent injury or damage being caused by straying animals. Yet everything depends on the extent to which the action of, say, a dog owner, in seeking to prevent his animal straying, is held by a court to be reasonable. Turning a dog out to enable it to be exercised off a leash and without a person in charge of it would most certainly be held to be unreasonable, especially if it was known that the dog had a tendency to chase horses. It would also be unreasonable to allow a dog to be out without proper supervision in an unfenced or inadequately fenced garden.

However, if a rider rode over private land without permission he would be trespassing, and the landowner would not be liable for accidents caused by a dog which was allowed to run freely there. The exception would be where there was a recognised bridlepath which crossed land, for such a path is dedicated for use by the public, including horse riders.

One of the problems in trying to bring a case against the owner of a dog which has caused an accident to either horse and/or rider by its behaviour is to know exactly who to sue. Under the Animals Act the keeper of a dog which trespasses and kills or injures livestock – which includes horses – can be either the actual owner or the person who has it in his care at the time of the trespass. It can also include the head of a household in which the person either owning or possessing the dog is under sixteen. The word 'possessing' is used in its widest context, not in terms of actual ownership but as having the dog under care and control at the time. If a dog worries a horse on agricultural land, under the Dogs (Protection of Livestock) Act 1953 an offence is committed not only by the dog's owner but the person who may have been in charge of it at that particular time. The question of who to sue and in what form a case should be brought is dealt with in Appendix I.

Riding accidents frequently occur in which motor vehicles are involved. If a vehicle collided with a horse and rider the outcome of a claim for damages would depend on whether or not the driver was negligent and could reasonably have foreseen the result of his conduct. Responsible drivers on seeing a horse being ridden on the highway would be expected to slow down and approach the animal with caution, common sense telling them that there is always the possibility that even a quiet, well-trained horse may take fright at too sudden a noise or a vehicle coming too close.

If an accident is caused as a result of a driver's negligence or lack of foresight as to the probable consequences of his actions, then the owner or rider of the horse would have a sound claim in law. If the rider did not own the horse but was injured as well as the horse, both rider and owner would have a claim.

This would apply with even more force if the driver either knew the district and was aware that it was a place where horses were ridden on the highway, or had passed a sign warning of the possibility of horses using the road. It goes without saying that a driver who sees ahead of him a rider of tender years should allow for the probability that a child is less experienced in handling a horse or pony than an adult.

If as a result of an accident the driver is prosecuted to conviction for an offence of reckless or careless driving, Section 11 of the Civil Evidence Act 1968 allows such a conviction to be admissable in civil proceedings that the offence has been committed, and might help in proving negligence.

It would be idle to pretend that either horses themselves or their riders, or a combination of both, do not cause accidents and under the Animals Act strict liability is imposed on owners of horses. This means that the person responsible for the horse

93

is also responsible and liable in law for any accident or damage it causes unless the damage was wholly due to the fault of the person suffering it or the risk was accepted voluntarily. However, an employee of a stable or riding school who is injured is not, in law, deemed to have voluntarily accepted the risk of injury. (Nor is an owner liable for injury to a trespasser caused by a horse kept in a field or stable.)

These defences are available only if the likelihood of the damage, or of its severity, is due to characteristics not normally found in animals of the same species, or at least only in particular circumstances or at particular times, and such characteristics were known to the horse's keeper or the person who had charge of it.

Riding schools

Anyone setting up a riding school must, on face value, be holding themselves out as experienced and competent to give riding instruction and this would apply for anyone employed for the same purpose. So through the doctrine of vicarious liability, the employer is usually responsible for the acts or omissions of his employees.

It is accepted in the eyes of the law that an employee is a person employed by another to do work under the direction and control of the employer as far as the manner in which the work is done, is concerned. This does not mean that the employer must be at the employee's elbow supervising the work at all times. This would be impossible in nearly all jobs let alone in a riding school.

An employer is also a person whose hours and conditions of work including rates of pay, are regulated by the employer.

There is a duty of care imposed on riding schools to teach in the proper manner. Indeed, a person who pays for a series of lessons is entering into a contractual relationship with the school and failure to teach that person properly would be a breach of contract, whether tuition was given by the principal of the school or an assistant.

Negligence comes into the way a person performs a contract

94

and in some circumstances, a riding school, if run as a limited company, or its principal, if a one-man concern, could, through one act of negligence, be guilty of both a breach of contract and a tort. This would happen if a riding school put a child up on a horse known to be totally unsuitable for a young person to handle, even when out with a qualified instructor, and the horse threw the child, bolted and caused injury to a third party.

The school could face two possible causes of action. One could be brought by the parent or guardian for damages for any injuries and/or shock that the child suffered; the second could be from the injured third party and would be in tort, the basis of which would be negligence. The injured third party could claim that the riding school was negligent in putting up a child on a horse it could not handle and that it should have reasonably foreseen the possibility of the horse getting out of hand and causing injury.

It could have been that the principal or the person in charge of the riding school was not on the premises at the time the child was put up on the horse and that the particular mount was chosen by an employee. In such a case the employer would be vicariously liable for the negligence of his employee. Similarly, if an employee failed to take proper care of a pupil in his charge and injury resulted, the employer would be just as responsible as if he had himself been giving tuition.

In the case of a livery stable which rented out horses, the owner of the stables could find himself in an invidious position. If he does not ask questions about the competence of a prospective rider, there is the possibility of his being held negligent if the horse provided is so unsuitable as to injure the rider. However, the defence of *volenti non fit injuria*, discussed earlier in this chapter, might well apply if the rider, for reasons best known to himself, chose a horse which he knew he could not handle. Obviously, if a rider overstated his own level of competence when asked about his experience, again the *volenti* principle would apply.

7 SETTING UP A RIDING ESTABLISHMENT

The owner of a riding establishment employs a number of part-time staff but, owing to sickness, is forced to leave the establishment in charge of a part-time worker aged fifteen for an hour on Saturday afternoon.

Is it legal?

Riding establishments need not be large; indeed, a person owning two horses and his own stabling might well decide to defray the expense of keeping the animals by giving riding lessons or hiring out the horses at times when he is not riding one or the other. This may be an activity which is carried out only at weekends or in the evenings but, nevertheless, if the hiring out is done by way of business it falls within the ambit of the Riding Establishments Act 1964.

On the other hand, a person may wish to build stables and open a riding establishment. The planning and building regulations have already been examined in Chapter 4. All that need be stated in this context is that if new stables are to be built, or existing buildings converted to stables, it is necessary to inquire of the local planning authority whether or not planning permission is required, and much will depend on the policy of the particular authority.

If permission is refused, there is a right of appeal to the Secretary of State for the Environment who may appoint an inspector to hold a public inquiry in which the appellant and the planning authority put their cases. There is always the possibility that even if the planning authority does not object, nearby residents might, and these objections could lead to the planning authority changing its mind with, again, the right of appeal.

If planning permission is necessary it will in all probability pay anyone contemplating setting up a business to engage the services of a local surveyor or architect, with knowledge of local planning requirements, who will prepare the application for planning permission, within whatever the appropriate local requirements may be.

Licensing

Having got over the planning hurdle, it is necessary to obtain a licence from the local authority to carry on the business of keeping horses for either the purpose of letting them out for hire or for use in giving riding instruction for payment, or both.

Section 6(4) of the Riding Establishments Act defines a horse as including any mare, gelding, pony, colt, filly or stallion as well as any mule, ass or jennet. The Act also says that a person shall be deemed to keep stables at the premises, which includes the land on which they stand, where horses employed for the business purposes mentioned above are kept.

So it will be seen that it is not necessary for the premises to be solely in the form of stables or a riding school. A farmer or landowner who keeps horses on his own premises for hiring out or lessons could be said to be running a riding establishment within the meaning of the Act.

There are a number of preconditions which have to be met before a licence is granted. First, the applicant must be at least eighteen years of age or an 'incorporated body', ie a company within the meaning of the varies Companies Acts or one which has been granted a Royal Charter. The establishment to be licensed must be within the area of the district council to which the application is being made and the necessary fee is paid. The stables, and any horses present, must also have been inspected by a vet who must then submit a report to the district council with sufficient particularity to enable the council to decide whether the stables and animals are suitable.

There is also one other important precondition: the applicant must not be disqualified from keeping a riding stable, a dog, pet shop, boarding kennels or from having the custody of animals. This condition is inserted solely to protect horses in the stables or riding school from being under the control of a person who is known to the courts for ill-treating animals in the past.

When deciding whether or not a licence will be granted, those responsible must have regard to the suitability and qualifications of the applicant to run a riding establishment, and in this they can be guided by the Act. One of the standards to be applied is the experience of the applicant in the management of horses. It might be necessary for the applicant to supply evidence of competence and this must inevitably be a subjective matter, unless the applicant is a holder of what the Act calls an approved certificate. In the latter case the need to prove experience in the management of horses will not be necessary and the legislation recognises as an approved certificate the following: an Assistant Instructor's Certificate of the British Horse Society; Instructor's Certificate and Fellowship of the same society; or Fellowship of the Institute of the Horse. The legislation also reserves the right to recognise any other certificate approved by the Secretary of State.

Even when all the preconditions and conditions are met, the district council issuing a licence must consider a number of other matters, all of which are for the benefit of the health and welfare of the horses to be stabled in the establishment. Section 4(b) of the Act states that, in deciding whether or not to grant a licence, the district council shall have regard to the need for securing:

(1) That paramount consideration will be given to the condition of horses and that they will be maintained in good health and in all respects physically fit and that, in the case of a horse kept for the purpose of its being let out on hire for riding or a horse kept for the purpose of it being used to provide instruction in riding, the horse will be suitable for the purpose for which it is kept;

(2) That the feet of all animals are properly trimmed and that, if shod, their shoes are properly fitted and in good condition;

(3) That there will be available at all times, accommodation for horses suitable as respects construction, size, number of occupants, lighting, ventilation, drainage and cleanliness and that these requirements be complied with not only in the case of new buildings but also in the case of buildings converted for use as stabling;

(4) That in the case of horses maintained at grass there will be available for them at all times during which they are so maintained adequate pasture and shelter and water and that supplementary feeds will be provided as and when required;

(5) That horses will be adequately supplied with suitable food, drink and (except in the case of horses maintained at grass so long as they are so maintained) bedding material, and will be adequately exercised, groomed and rested and visited at suitable intervals;

(6) That all resonable precautions will be taken to prevent and control the spread among horses of infectious or contagious diseases and that veterinary first aid equipment and medicines shall be provided and maintained in the premises;

(7) That appropriate steps will be taken for protection and extrication of horses in case of fire and, in particular, that the name, address

and telephone number of the licence holder or some other responsible person will be kept displayed in a prominent position on the outside of the premises and that instructions as to action to be taken in the event of fire, with particular regard to the extrication of horses, will be kept displayed in a prominent position on the outside of the premises;

(8) That adequate accommodation will be provided for forage, bedding, stable equipment and saddlery.

This particular section of the Act also empowers the district council to specify such conditions in the granting of the licence which may be necessary to see that all or any of the above requirements are met. In addition the Riding Establishments Act does not specify the number of hours a horse may be worked and it is likely that in this matter a local authority would impose its own working hours' regulations.

These requirements spell out, in terms which brook no misunderstanding, to would-be holders of riding establishment licences what is considered necessary for the health and welfare of animals in their charge. But this legislation does not cover establishments which provide nothing else but livery in the sense of care and accommodation. This may be a strange omission – as boarding kennels, catteries and pet shops need to be licensed – unless those responsible for the legislation were of the opinion that such livery establishments either did not exist or were insignificant in number and that owners of horses at livery could sue for breach of contract if there was any question of negligence. Furthermore, there is the additional protection as far as horses are concerned provided by legislation specifically aimed at stamping out cruelty to and ill-treatment of animals.

The Act also contains a number of penal offences for which the punishment is a fine or up to three months' imprisonment or both. Offences under Section 3 are created if the owner of a riding establishment:

(1) At a time when a horse is in such a condition that its riding would be likely to cause suffering to the horse, lets out the horse on hire or uses it for the purpose of providing, in return for payment,

instruction in riding or for the purpose of demonstrating riding; lets out on hire for riding or uses for the purpose of providing, in return for payment, instruction in riding or demonstrating riding any horse aged three years or under or any mare heavy with foal or any mare within three months after foaling;

(2) Supplies for a horse which is let out on hire for riding, equipment which is used in the course of the hiring and suffers, at the time when it is supplied, from a defect of such a nature as to be apparent on inspection and as to be likely to cause suffering to the horse or an accident to the rider;

(3) Fails to provide such curative care as may be suitable if any, for a sick or injured horse which is kept with a view to its being let out on hire or used for a purpose mentioned in paragraph 1 above;

(4) In keeping a riding establishment knowingly permits any person who is for the time being disqualified under the Act from keeping a riding establishment;

(5) With intent to avoid inspection under the Act, conceals or causes to be concealed, any horse maintained by the riding establishment.

There is a further offence created which carries similar penalties of a fine or imprisonment or both. This covers a person who, for the purpose of obtaining a licence under the Act, gives false information or recklessly makes a false statement. It will be seen by the way this offence is described, that it covers not only a person who knowingly gives wrong information but the person who recklessly makes a false statement, ie without caring whether it is false or not. It is also an offence, carrying a modest fine, wilfully to obstruct or delay a person exercising his powers under the Act.

Of particular interest is the offence under (2) above of sending out a horse and rider with tack which is obviously defective and which leads to an accident to the rider and suffering to the horse. It is not difficult to conceive that such defective tack could cause the rider to fall and, if a prosecution was to follow, proof of a conviction for this offence would be more than helpful to a rider seeking compensation from the owners of the establishment for injury.

Under the Act a district council can authorise in writing any one of its officers, or an officer of any other local authority, a veterinary surgeon and a veterinary practitioner (in law there is a difference between the two) to inspect any premises in its area including land where there is reason to believe a person is keeping a riding establishment, or an establishment which is already licenced or has applied for the grant of a licence. Before such an appointed person can enter an establishment, he has to produce his written authority if it is requested and can only carry out his inspection at what the Act describes as 'reasonable times'. Obviously, reasonable times are likely to be during normal working hours. The authority extends to the inspection of horses and anything on the premises for the purpose of discovering whether an offence has been, or is being, committed.

There is a curious exception in this section of the Act in as much as it appears from the way it is drafted that, although authority is granted to enter unlicensed riding establishments, there is no need to make a report – which might be because the very fact that an unlicensed establishment is operating is an offence in itself.

In the event of an offence being committed under the Act a local authority – defined as a council of a district or of a London borough, or the Common Council of the City of London – may authorise a prosecution in the local magistrates' court. But if the offence concerns contravention of, or non-compliance with, a condition on which the licence was granted and can be said generally to refer to the welfare of horses in the establishment, no prosecution may start until the local authority has received and considered a veterinary report.

There is one other section of the Act of vital importance as it is further concerned with the welfare of horses as well as affording protection to members of the public using facilities offered by the establishment.

(1) A horse found on inspection of the premises by an authorised officer to be in need of veterinary attention shall not be returned to work until the holder of the licence has obtained at his own expense and has lodged with the local authority a veterinary certificate that the horse is fit for work;

(2) No horse will be let out on hire for riding or used for providing instruction in riding without supervision by a responsible person of the age of sixteen years or over unless (in the case of a horse let out for hire for riding) the holder of the licence is satisfied that the hirer of the horse is competent to ride without supervision;

(3) The carrying on of the business of a riding establishment shall at no time be left in the charge of any person under sixteen years of age;

(4) The licence holder shall hold a current insurance policy which insures him against liability for any injury sustained by those who hire a horse from him for riding and those who use a horse in the course of receiving from him, in return for payment, instruction in riding and arising out of the hire or use of the horse as aforesaid and which also insures such persons in respect of any liability which may be incurred by them in respect of injury to any person caused by, or arising out of, the hire or use of the horse as aforesaid;

(5) A register shall be kept by the licence holder of all horses in his possession aged three years and under and usually kept on the premises which shall be available for inspection by an authorised officer at all reasonable times.

These conditions are basic to any licence, with or without additional conditions which may be applied by the licencing authority.

As has been noted earlier, one of the factors the district council will take into account before granting a licence is the competence of the applicant. So, it must be assumed that the holder of the licence has some knowledge which enables him to tell whether or not a horse is in need of veterinary attention, as required by the first of the implied conditions. Obviously, as a prosecution based on what might be called the health and welfare of a particular horse can only be brought after a local authority has considered a veterinary report, it would be equable on the part of an authority not to bring a prosecution if a horse was suffering from a condition or disease which could be diagnosed only by a veterinarian. It is to be hoped that those who run riding establishments, and have a working knowledge of equine ailments, would summon professional help at the first sign of something being physically wrong.

The second implied condition is basic commonsense as far as

the danger it seeks to avoid is concerned. Nevertheless, it may create a problem for the licence holder of a riding establishment for that person – or one of his staff for whom he is vicariously liable in law – must take a subjective view of the competence of anyone to ride without supervision. The very young rider will in all probability be in need of supervision. One sign of the competence or otherwise of a rider may well be the ease with which he gets into the saddle; but even a person who mounts without difficulty may not be sufficiently experienced to ride safely on busy roads or at speed over a particular stretch of countryside. So where a rider unknown to the licence holder or his staff wishes to hire a horse, it is essential that that person's ability should be established if an offence is not to be committed.

The condition requiring insurance needs no comment except to note that it covers third party liability. The last of the implied conditions – the need to keep a register of horses under three years of age – again underlines the concern of the Act for the welfare of horses in riding establishments.

Finally, it must be noted as far as conditions are concerned that not only does a court have the power to fine or imprison on conviction for offences under the Act, but also the power to cancel a licence to run a riding establishment. This may disqualify the offender from keeping a riding establishment for such a period as the court thinks fit. In theory this could mean disqualification for life although, if such a Draconian ban was imposed, a crown court, to whom all appeals under the Act may be made, might think such a disqualification too long and substitute a fixed term. If disqualification is ordered, the magistrates' court may, if it thinks fit, suspend the order pending an appeal.

A licence holder may also be disqualified if he is convicted of any offence under the Protection of Animals Act 1911, or the Protection of Animal Boarding Establishments Act 1963.

The fee payable for a licence is determined by the individual authority and each licence covers the year for which it was granted, or the following year, and remains in force for one

SETTING UP A RIDING ESTABLISHMENT

year. Should the licence holder die, the Act states that the licence is treated as having been granted to his personal representatives and it will remain in force for three months following the death. The Act also empowers the council to extend and re-extend the three months' period if satisfied that the extension is necessary to wind up the estate and there are no circumstances which make it undesirable.

Care of visitors
There are matters to be considered by those who run riding establishments which involve legal responsibilities towards their employees and visitors to the stables.

A general outline of employment law is dealt with in Chapter 8, but there are two points which can be discussed appropriately here. One is the responsibility of the employer for the acts of an employee, which is known as vicarious liability. This imposes on the employer civil liability for any damage or civil wrongs done by the employee in the course of his employment and, in some circumstances, for any criminal acts. Injuries to third parties caused by acts of employees in the course of their work in all probability will be covered by insurance (see Chapter 9).

But there is a specific piece of legislation – the Employers' Liability (Compulsory Insurance) Act 1969 – the title of which really speaks for itself, which was passed to ensure that all employees were covered in respect of insurance for any injury they might suffer during the course of their employment.

In the case of riding establishments there are a number of risks for employees, many of which can be obviated or mitigated if correct instruction is given, so it is important for the employer that such instructions are given as and when necessary. One reason is that if, after being instructed in the correct way of doing a job, the employee for some reason best known to himself does it incorrectly, a court might hold this to be contributory negligence and damages would be reduced accordingly.

Owners of riding establishments should also be aware of their legal responsibilities under the Occupiers Liability Act 1957. Although under the Riding Establishments Act 1964 it is an offence for a licence holder not to be insured against third party liability this refers only to liability sustained while clients are out riding or receiving instruction. It does not cover accidents which may occur in the yard or the office, not only to potential customers but to any person with a right to be on the premises, which includes tradesmen and sales representatives as well as persons invited to the establishment for, say, social purposes.

Basically the Act imposes on the occupier the responsibility for seeing that visitors are safe while on the premises – and stables may be more risky places than other commercial premises. It is essential not only that the premises be structurally sound so that injury is not caused to visitors, but also that a visitor does not come to harm through the negligence of the occupier or his staff – for instance, by tripping over rakes and brooms left carelessly placed.

If a visitor is injured as the result of faulty workmanship by an outside contractor, the owner of the establishment will not be liable if he can prove he had taken all reasonable care to make certain that the work was done by a competent contractor and carried out in a proper manner. The liability would then fall on to the contractor. This means that when any work is carried out it is wise to use a contractor who belongs to his own trade association, such membership being some indication of competence and standing, or is skilled by reason of many years' experience in his particular trade. This effectively cuts out, if the defence is to be relied upon, what can best be described as 'cowboy contractors' and those offering a service at a cut price. A court is likely to take the view that a reasonable man should have realised that cut price can often be equated with lower standards of performance.

A higher standard of care is also expected to be shown by occupiers towards children, and even trespassers are entitled to a measure of protection under the Act. Trespassers may enter premises at their own risk but the occupier is expected to show humanity and is not entitled to set traps or other devices which may cause injury.

In these days of vandalism it is not unexpected for occupiers of premises, especially those such as stables which may be left unattended at night, to keep guard dogs. Although these animals are now quite commonplace, in the late 1960s and 1970s this was not the case and there were many cases of innocent persons being savaged. As a result the Guard Dogs Act was passed in 1975 which defined a guard dog as being one used to protect premises, persons guarding premises and property to be found on premises. So what constitutes premises under this particular piece of legislation?

For a start the Act defines premises as land which is not used for agricultural purposes or is within the bounds of a dwelling house. So stables on agricultural land which form part of a farm or smallholding would be exempted from the provisions of the Act, as would stables within the boundary of a dwelling house. Agricultural land is also defined as land which is a meadow or is used for, among other purposes, grazing. But there are a large number of stables and riding establishments which in all probability do not fall into the two categories which grant exemption.

It is an offence to keep a guard dog on such premises, or permit it to be kept, unless there is a handler who is capable of controlling the animal or it is so secured so that it is not free to roam. Obviously a dog on the end of a chain which gave it limited liberty could not be said to be capable of roaming the stables. There is also an obligation under the Act for premises where there are guard dogs to display a notice to this effect.

At this stage consideration needs to be given to how far a person can go in protecting his property. Undoubtedly stables and similar establishments will contain valuable horses and expensive tack, and as, in many cases, stables will be situated in quiet rural areas with easy access, they could be a prime target for thieves and vandals.

One thing that is quite certain is that a would-be thief or vandal who enters premises without lawful authority is guilty of burglary under the Theft Act 1968 and the law permits an occupier to use reasonable force to evict trespassers after they have been asked, and have refused, to leave. The problem is defining 'reasonable force', and much would depend on the actions of the trespasser. A trespasser who refuses to leave may be physically ejected with no more force than is necessary and a court would take into account, in deciding whether or not force was reasonable, the physical strength of the intruder.

Probably an occupier is not entitled to use a weapon against an unarmed intruder and a well-muscled occupier who uses all his attributes and strength against a weaker intruder would probably not be said to be using reasonable force. When dealing with intruders a fine balance has to be struck and if life and property can be protected without recourse to violence so much the better.

8 RUNNING A BUSINESS

Two friends set up a small riding school in
partnership, one putting in more money
than the other. Their friendship fell apart
when the one who put up less money left
the neighbourhood and demanded an equal
share of the profits.

What, in law, was that person's legal right?

Whether a person is running a riding school, or stables from which horses are hired out, or just providing livery, the venture is presumably being run as a business with the objective of providing a living for the owner.

There are three main ways in which a business can be run: as a sole proprietor, a partnership or a limited company. All have distinct advantages, all some disadvantages, and it is up to the individuals involved to decide which way is most suitable having weighed up all relevant factors and taken, it is hoped, the advice of an accountant and/or a solicitor.

Running a business as a sole proprietor

The easiest method is to set up business on one's own account, paying tax and national insurance as a self-employed person and registering for VAT if the projected turnover is likely to be above the amount for which registration is necessary. (No figure is quoted here as it is one HM Customs and Excise, which is responsible for VAT, can vary, usually in an upward direction.) Providing the person setting up a riding or livery establishment has either stables already available or sufficient capital or access to money to buy or lease stables, he could be in business the day after a licence has been granted.

The raising of capital is, of course, the necessary prerequisite of most small businesses and the obvious place to raise it, if there are insufficient private means, is a person's own bank. Subject to the plans for the new establishment not being long on flights of fancy and short on reality, and with a sensible cash flow projection, a bank may well be sympathetic to an approach for a loan to start the business.

It will require security and this is usually likely to take the form of a legal charge on property owned by the borrower. If the borrower owns his own stables and land a bank may consider this to be sufficient security: if not, the bank will almost certainly want to put a legal charge on any other property owned by the borrower and this is likely to be his own home.

If the home is already mortgaged it will be necessary for the building society, or other financial institution holding the first mortgage, to give permission for a further charge to be placed on the property. Whether or not permission is granted will depend on the amount outstanding on the first loan and the value of the property which will form the security. If a bank has to place a legal charge on domestic property, it will wish to examine the title deeds.

If the house is in the joint names of husband and wife, both will have to agree to the second charge. Similarly, if the house is only in the name of either the husband or the wife, the lender will require both husband and wife to sign the necessary documents. This is because even if the house is in the name of only one spouse the law frequently holds that the other has an equitable interest in the matrimonial home. Any pledge on the home is invalid without the consent and full understanding of the other spouse for the charge to be imposed. This will be the only legal formality required if money is to be borrowed and the sole proprietor is ready for business.

At one time, if the business was to be run under a name which was not that of the proprietor, the name had to be registered. Now if a business name is used all that is necessary is for the letterheads, bills, receipts, etc, to have the name and permanent address of where the business operates to enable correspondence to be sent to the correct place.

The main disadvantage of running a business as a sole proprietor lies in the event of failure. No one setting up a riding establishment should do so without undertaking research to find out whether or not such a service is needed in a particular area. Unfortunately circumstances change and there is always the risk of any number of unforeseen events turning a profitable business venture into one losing money. If this should happen the sole proprietor is very much at risk as he alone is responsible for debts incurred by the business, and in extreme cases he can be made bankrupt and his possessions, including perhaps his home, seized to satisfy creditors.

Partnerships

Another way of running a business, which might seem particularly attractive to friends who share a genuine love of horses and equine pursuits, is a partnership – defined in the Partnership Act 1890 as a relationship existing between persons carrying on a business in common with a view to profit.

Many partnerships started by friends to profit out of a common interest begin with high hopes and end in deep despair. There is a world of difference between two or more people sharing a love of riding and meeting regularly to ride out together or mingle socially, and these same people working together day in day out in running a business for profit. From this point of view alone, partnerships should be approached with caution and partnership agreements never entered into until all potential partners have sought legal advice and a partnership agreement drawn up.

Unless there is an agreement to the contrary, the Partnership Act states that all profits must be shared equally, as must the losses, and each partner can look to the other for indemnity for any purchases made on behalf of the business. It could well be that one partner is able to put more money or money's-worth into the partnership business than the other. If this is the case, does the party who put up more get a proportionately bigger share of the profits? And how much is a partner to take out of the business each week? These are two common matters which may arise and unless there is agreement on such matters at the time a partnership is created, the seeds of discontent may be sown.

Other points to be kept in mind are: what happens when another person is invited to become a partner; pension provisions for partners; and whether one partner is to have a casting vote if a decision vital to the development of the business is to be taken. This last point is particularly important if such a development involves an additional financial burden in the intitial stages on members of the partnership.

These reservations should not be taken as expressing a view that partnerships are trouble-prone and even doomed to failure.

On the contrary, partnerships flourish in may walks of life and this can be helped by a proper partnership agreement being drawn up by a solicitor. Such an agreement should not only incorporate the points referred to above but also take into consideration provisions for one or more of the partners leaving through retirement, ill health, moving away from the district or other causes which may not have been envisaged at the time those people with a common interest in horses and riding decided to band together to go into business.

Forming a limited company

The third way of going into business, either with members of one's family or with friends, is to form a limited company, which is a comparatively straightforward and simple procedure and can be carried out at no great expense by an accountant or solicitor.

A limited company is a separate legal entity and responsible for its own debts and, as was seen in the previous chapter, is entitled to hold a licence to run a riding establishment. To what extent a company is capitalised depends on how much those forming it wish to put in. Many small companies have a nominal share capital of only £100 with only two £1 shares issued, possibly, if it is a family affair, to the two directors. This means that the company has the minimum amount of capitalisation, and this negligible sum is not likely to impress other businesses with whom a line of credit may be desired. On the other hand, if those forming the company wish to put up, say, £10,000, this can be done by capitalising the company at this sum with the shares distributed usually in proportion to the amount individual shareholders put up.

Because a limited company is responsible for its own debts, if it should be unfortunate enough to have to go into liquidation because of its inability to meet its obligations, all the investors lose is their original investment if they have paid for their shares in full. If they have only paid, for example, 50p for each £1 share they hold, in the event of compulsory winding up – when a creditor petitions a court for an order to this effect because of the debtor company's inability to pay what it owes – the shareholders will be called upon to pay the balance of money owed on each share.

Companies fall into two categories – private and public limited companies – but for the purpose of this book only private companies will be discussed and there are a number of legal requirements which have to be fulfilled whatever the capitalisation of a private company may be.

When a company is formed, certain essential documents have to be lodged with the Registrar of Companies. They are:

The Memorandum of Association.
The Articles of Association.
Statement of authorised share capital.
A statutory declaration that all the requirements of the various Companies Acts have been met.

At this point a closer look at what is involved in, and the importance of, the first two documents is necessary. The Memorandum of Association has to state the name of the company and whether the registered office is situated in England and Wales or Scotland. There is no statutory need for the registered office to be situated at the riding establishment, although this may be the most convenient place. It is quite a common practice for the registered office of a small private company to be that of the accountant to the company.

The most important part of the Memorandum of Association is that which describes the objects of the company. Obviously with a riding establishment the main objects will be to carry on a business of: providing horses for the purpose of hiring out to riders; providing horses and instructors for lessons in riding; and providing a livery for rent for people to lodge their horses.

These three objects would in many cases be sufficient to meet the initial needs of a private company set up for such purposes, but it is necessary to look ahead. Hopefully a company will be successful and expand. It might wish to add horse transportation to its activities or to become a forage merchant. Unless the Memorandum of Association is widely drawn to

116

permit these extra activities a company which does so is said to be acting *ultra vires* – that is, beyond its legal powers.

Until quite recently a company seeking to enter into business contracts which were outside the scope of its objects could have been penalised by such contracts being declared by a court as unenforceable. However, under the European Communities Act 1972 a contract which would otherwise have been unenforceable can be enforced if the other party acted in good faith, although it would remain unenforceable on the part of the company which, by entering into it, was acting beyond its powers.

The Memorandum of Association also has to state the amount of the company's share capital and, perhaps most important for the shareholders, that liability is limited.

The Articles of Association set out how the company is to be run, what the voting rights of shareholders are, the provisions for holding meetings of the company, and what powers are invested in directors and how they can be removed.

There are further provisions in the Articles of Association which, in their way, are as important as the objects of the company contained in the Memorandum of Association. The first is the power of the company to borrow money, for unless this is stated a company would be acting beyond its powers if it borrowed money for expansion or other business purposes. Even if a company does have powers of borrowing, a bank might still require directors to give personal guarantees if the company has insufficient tangible assets on which a legal charge can be put as security.

The other important provision is that outlining how shares are to be transferred. Many small private companies have been founded by one person with members of his or her family becoming shareholders and, in all probability, working directors. The founder of such a company may, not unnaturally, wish to keep the shares either within the family circle or the family of friends who might have invested originally.

Because a share is a tangible asset even though it may have

less than its face value, it can be sold, given away, bequeathed and assigned, and in a family-run, close-knit business, it may be essential that any shareholder with a good-size holding should not dispose of it outside the family circle. This can be assured only by stating in the Articles of Association that any shareholder wishing to dispose of his equity must either offer it first to existing shareholders or get their approval before disposing of his shares outside the immediate family.

In any small private company directors will be taking an active part in its management. In the case of riding establishments of any description it is more than likely that one or two of the directors will actively manage the stables and give lessons, and the legal duties imposed on them as directors will not prove onerous or too time consuming.

Legally, a director is an officer of the company and is responsible for its day-to-day running. In the small company a director is almost certain to be an employee as well as a shareholder. Indeed, there may well be tax advantages in this method and to comply with the Companies Act 1967, a copy of his contract of service must be available for inspection by shareholders if he is an executive – that is, working – director.

Every company must have a company secretary who is legally responsible for its administration. He takes minutes of board and annual meetings, deals with registering share transactions and signs the annual returns. In most family-run companies, the post of company secretary is usually held by a director who thus has two roles.

The annual returns are not too off-putting. Within seven months from the end of a company's financial year, its annual accounts, signed by directors and certified by a chartered accountant, have to be sent to the Registrar of Companies – there are penalties for not complying – together with a return showing any change of directors or shareholders.

There are provisions for removing directors under the Companies Act 1948. Under an Act of the same name, passed in 1976, a director may be restrained by a court from being involved in the management of a company if that person has been persistently late in submitting the statutory annual returns. Under the 1948 Act an undischarged bankrupt is barred from the management of a company while he remains a bankrupt.

Nevertheless, it will be seen that if the basic essentials, such as the terms to be contained in the Memorandum and Articles of Association, are got right initially and the annual returns made within the specified time limits, running a small limited company is not a difficult task.

Employment law
There are certain legal obligations imposed by law on employers with regard to their employees and it is more than likely that even a small establishment will employ one or two people.

Juveniles
Many stables and riding establishments employ juveniles in a part-time capacity. For youngsters with a passion for horses and riding this is an ideal arrangement, giving them the opportunity to learn more about horses and how to keep tack in good condition, with the possibility of free riding from time to time.

There are stringent regulations covering the employment of juveniles which proprietors of stables and riding establishments can easily be in breach of through ignorance rather than intention. The first fact to keep in mind is that no child under thirteen years of age can be employed, and children between thirteen and sixteen are restricted to being allowed to work for no more than two hours a day on a normal school day. The two hours can be between either 7 and 8 am or 5 and 7 pm – the time when a young person is most likely to wish to work with horses.

Less strict, however, are the regulations covering Saturdays and school holidays. Though the prohibition remains against juveniles working before 7 am and after 7 pm, they can work a maximum of four hours a day if under fifteen and eight hours if between fifteen and sixteen. Work on Sundays for juveniles is restricted to two hours a day and only between 7 and 10 am.

There is also a restriction on the type of work a juvenile can do and this can be described best as a bar on heavy physical work, including the lifting of heavy weights, in the course of employment. It therefore becomes a matter of debate as to whether or not lifting a bale of hay would fall into this category. Indeed, it is a matter of subjective judgement, for much would depend on the person lifting the bale. What would not be a heavy weight for a strapping six-footer might impose strain on a slighter, less well built person.

The regulations covering the employment of juveniles are enforced by the local authority. It is wise for anyone employing a juvenile for the first time to check that there are no variations on what can be called the standard regulations in their particular area.

Young people between the ages of sixteen and eighteen are treated almost as adults for employment purposes but there are still some restrictions. Working hours may be no more than nine in any one day or forty-eight in any one week; overtime is restricted to cases of emergency and seasonal work and, again, it is a matter of judgement on the part of the employer as to what work in stables or riding establishments falls into these two categories.

Most of the law about employment of juveniles may be found in the Young Persons (Employment) Acts 1938 and 1964. Offences are punishable by a fine on conviction in a magistrates' court.

Terms of employment

When an employee is taken on, a contract exists between that employee and the employer and each owes to the other rights and responsibilities. Because it was considered essential that there should be no misunderstanding about what were or were not the terms of employment, the Employment Protection (Consolidation) Act 1978 laid on the employer the duty to provide, within thirteen weeks of an employee starting work, a written statement setting out a number of important facts.

The statement, which need not be provided if all the relevant facts are contained in a letter formally offering the job to a potential employee, must outline: the hours to be worked; the pay, how it is to be made and at what intervals – weekly, monthly, etc, the date of commencement of employment; whether any previous service is to count as continuous employment for the purpose of redundancy payment or other benefits; if overtime is compulsory or not; details of holiday entitlement and pay; the employee's entitlement to be paid during the periods of sickness or injury; any pension scheme which may be operating; the job title; and, although unlikely to affect small stables and riding establishments, disciplinary rules and procedure and who an employee should talk to in the event of any grievance. Finally, the contract of employment must also specify length of notice. Employees are entitled to a statutory minimum as follows: for employment of more than one month but less than two years, one week; two to twelve years of service, one week for each full year of employment; and over twelve years, three months' notice. Naturally, an employer is entitled to give an employee the appropriate salary in lieu of notice.

Even the way in which wages are paid is regulated. Manual workers, and anyone employed to muck out and keep stables clean would fall into this category, are entitled to be paid in cash while an employer is authorised by the Payment of Wages by Cheque Act 1960 to insist on other staff receiving wages by cheque. Under this Act manual workers may request in writing payment by cheque.

Furthermore, every employee, however he is paid, has to be given a statement of his pay which must be itemised to show the gross pay, net pay and not only deductions that have been made but why they have been made. In practice this will normally be for income tax, national insurance and any contributions for a pension scheme. It is unlawful for an employer to deduct money for the provision of any safety equipment or clothing which has to be provided under the Health and Safety at Work Act 1974.

When dealing with the law as it affects employment, it is necessary to decide whether or not a person is in fact employed and has a contract of service as distinct from a contract for service. An employee in the accepted sense of the word has a contract of service under which, in return for pay and other benefits, he is under the control in general terms of his employer.

An independent contractor holds a contract for service and this could apply to a person who is engaged in what is commonly termed a freelance capacity to give a certain number of hours of riding lessons each week. While such a person may have an agreed fee for each lesson, he will not be entitled to the benefits which accrue under employment law to an employee.

Thus it can probably be argued that a skilled rider who keeps a horse at a riding school free of charge in return for giving a certain number of riding lessons each week, either with or without payment, is not an employee in the legal sense of the word as it would be up to the particular rider to decide how best to give lessons. On the other hand, undoubtedly a contract exists between such a person and the establishment but it is not one of employment.

The employer's responsibilities

The previously mentioned Health and Safety at Work Act also plays an important part in that body of law which can be termed as employment which, among other things, lays on employers the following responsibilities:

, To ensure, as far as reasonably practical, the health and safety of employees while at work.

To make sure that visitors and others who are not employees are not unreasonably exposed to risks which affect their health and safety.

To ensure that entrances and exits are safe and do not constitute a risk to health.

To provide the necessary instruction, training and supervision to ensure the safety, health and welfare of employees.

There are other points, but the above are judged to be those most likely to affect stables and riding establishments. The first really needs no explanation; the second reinforces the obligation placed on occupiers under the Occupiers Liability Act which has already been discussed in Chapter 7. A little more consideration is needed when discussing the need to make certain that exits and entrances are safe.

Many stables and riding schools are situated off the main highway and are approached by made-up or unmade roads. Such is the wide interpretation that courts have given to the words 'entrances and exits' that it is not impossible for such a road to be included under this definition. So it behoves the owner of a riding establishment to make sure that any approach road is kept as safe as is reasonably possible in all the circumstances.

The same applies to the maintenance of stables premises. As already observed, rakes and brooms left lying about can be a cause of accidents. And in inclement weather owners should do all they can to make sure that stable yards are not dangerously slippery with ice or impacted snow.

The last of the employers' obligations quoted above – the need to provide necessary instruction and supervision – places a greater onus on those who run stables, etc, then perhaps on other businesses. Such instruction must be given, when needed, in the handling of horses, including the safest way of entering a particular box, and in feeding and grooming.

The Act does not apply to stables and riding establishments which are on agricultural land. This re-opens the argument of whether or not such establishments on farms or smallholdings are separate businesses or part and parcel of whatever form of agriculture or horticulture is undertaken on the land in question.

Enforcement of the Act lies with the Health and Safety Executive and local authorities, who have the power of entering and inspecting premises and serving notices on employers to rectify anything which may be a danger to workers.

Dismissing staff

The law as it relates to dismissing employees and redundancy can be a veritable minefield for the unwary. For a start every employee with more than twenty-six weeks' service is entitled to be told in writing of the reasons for his dismissal, and in the case of a stable or riding establishment with a staff of less than twenty, employees have a legal right not to be dismissed unfairly after 104 consecutive weeks of employment. These conditions apply to part-time workers as well as those employed full time though only to part-timers who have worked between eight and sixteen hours a week in the past five consecutive years. When an employee is given notice it is of great importance that the correct period of notice – or money in lieu – as outlined earlier in this chapter, is given.

Some youngsters enter into what, at its best, can be called an informal arrangment whereby they undertake a prescribed course and receive tuition and a small sum in return for carrying out stable duties.

Obviously they cannot be said to be in part-time employment so would not be covered as far as redundancy, etc, is concerned under existing law. Such persons would, of course, have the protection of legislation covering health and safety at work.

Most likely a contractual situation would exist between the pupil and a riding establishment and any protection would depend on the terms of the contract.

The concept of unfair dismissal was introduced into employment law in 1971 and means, in fact, that every employee, subject to time limits referred to above, has the right in law not to be dismissed unfairly. There are five grounds which are recognised in law as fair dismissal:

Lack of capability or qualification on the part of an employee to do the job for which he was engaged.
Misconduct.
When continued employment would be in breach of the law.
Redundancy.
Other substantial reasons.

As there is most likely to have to be over two years' consecutive work by an employee in the average riding establishment, it is inconceivable that the first ground would apply as the shortcomings of such an employee would be found out within a matter of weeks of taking up employment.

Misconduct covers a multitude of sins and not just dishonesty *vis-à-vis* the employer. In the context of a riding establishment it would undoubtedly include cruelty towards horses and ponies and possibly rudeness or bad manners towards riders using the establishment.

Continued employment in breach of the law would apply to riding establishments if, for example, a manager was employed who became a disqualified person on conviction of offences outlined in the Riding Establishments Act, or if a person was employed to drive a horse box having lost his licence for a period of time.

Before an employer dismisses an employee on the grounds of redundancy, there have to be reasons to justify such an action. It is no good seeking to get rid of an unwanted worker on the grounds of redundancy if genuine grounds do not exist.

In general, redundancy will be held to be genuine if one or all of the following conditions exist:

The employee or employees is or are put on part-time work or laid off.
The business is sold.
The business moves its location.
All or part of the business closes.

Obviously if there is insufficient work for an employee in a stable or riding establishment to do and that person is put on part time or laid off, this could well come under the description of economic necessity which might be held to be a 'substantial reason' referred to below.

An establishment which is flourishing may wish to increase its business and this might mean leaving existing stables and moving elsewhere. In most circumstances it is inconceivable that such a move would be very far away from the original stables and the area which has proved to be successful, so an employee who tried to claim redundancy payments on the grounds that his place of employment had moved would stand very little chance unless the new place of employment was some miles away.

If a riding establishment is sold and employees dismissed, redundancy payments have to be made but if the same jobs are offered at the same terms by the new owner there is no redundancy and it is usual, in circumstances such as these, for length of service with the old employer to count with the new.

When it is necessary to pay redundancy there is a method of computing the amount due to each individual employee based on the age and number of years of service in excess of two years. No account is taken of service before the age of eighteen or over the age of sixty-five in the case of men and sixty for women. There are financial limits on the amount of payment, which is laid down by the Department of Employment and reviewed each year. If the owner of a riding establishment wishes to reclaim up to 35 per cent of any redundancy payments from the Government, it is essential that the correct procedure is followed and the proper forms submitted. Only establishments employing less than ten people are allowed to reclaim a portion of redundancy payments. Advice and forms can be obtained from any local office of the Department of Employment.

The fifth ground for fair dismissal, 'other substantial reasons', can create many problems for there is no yardstick or even rule of thumb by which a substantial reason can be measured. Much will depend on what an industrial tribunal, which hears claims by employees for compensation for unfair dismissal, considers to be substantial. Some have held that if a business is going through a bad financial period, this in itself is a substantial reason. And it could be that a person who became a disruptive influence on other staff could be dismissed fairly. What is crystal clear is that no one may be dismissed on the grounds of their sex, race or trade union activities.

Despite the introduction of the concept of unfair dismissal into law, there is a further remedy open to an employee in certain circumstances. This is a civil action for wrongful dismissal which will be heard in either the High Court or a county court, dependent upon the amount of money claimed. This action is based on breach of contract between employer and employee and, unlike unfair dismissal, there is no minimum period of employment before which a claim can be brought.

If an employee feels that he has a case to bring an action for unfair dismissal this will be heard by a local industrial tribunal. Such a tribunal has a legally qualified chairman and two other members, one of whom will be a representative of management and the other, usually, of a trade union. Hearings are usually informal and if the finding is in favour of the employee, a monetary award is made. This award takes into account the age and length of service of the employee and compensation for loss suffered as a result of the unfair dismissal. In some circumstances the tribunal will order the employee to be reinstated and if this is not done further compensation is payable.

9 INSURANCE

Because standard equine policies did not give all the cover an owner who took part in equestrian events required, he went to an insurance broker with a list of eventualities he wished to insure against. When one of the eventualities arose he found out he was not in fact covered.

What can he do?

Insurance is compulsory under the Riding Establishments Act and the Employers' Liability (Compulsory Insurance) Act, and individual horse owners usually wish to take out cover against third party liability, death or injury to their horses and themselves. There are companies specialising in insurance of horses and riders and their policies are likely to cover all or some of the following eventualities:

Accident and injury to, or sickness or disease of the horse or pony.
Death of the horse or pony from any cause.
Loss of horse or pony by theft or straying.
Any accident involving a third party or parties.
Loss or theft of tack.
Death or injury of the rider.
Loss or damage to a trap, cart or trailer.

It is a regrettable fact that many people in all walks of life, and not just those connected with horses, never take the trouble of reading what is commonly referred to as the small print. Not until the need for insurance arises do they discover that they are not either fully or partially covered for the eventuality.

It must be stressed that an insurance policy is a contract known to the law as one which demands *uberrimae fidei*, that is a contract calling for good faith on the part of the person seeking insurance. This means that it is essential that there is full and frank disclosure of all relevant facts and honest answers given to the questions asked in the proposal form. It would be impossible for an insurance company to check the truth or otherwise of every answer on a proposal form; and it is only on the strength of those answers that a company can decide whether or not it wishes to accept the risk and, if it does, if it should be at its usual premium or higher because of the particular circumstances disclosed.

Those who live in certain parts of London which are high risk areas because of burglaries are likely to find that unless they take stringent security precautions, on a pound for pound value, their premiums will be considerably higher than those applying to a rural residence; just as a car parked in the street in central London will attract a far higher premium than one kept in a garage in the suburbs.

Insurance companies, and especially those which specialise in equine and related policies, are astute at assessing risks on a general basis but, obviously, they are not in a position to assess the risk or risks inherent in every individual policy issued. Failure to disclose facts relevant to the risk could and probably would result in the policy being voided if such lack of disclosure or an untrue answer is discovered. Furthermore, although for convenience an insurance company may not require a form to be completed when the policy comes up for renewal each year, there is a duty on the insured person to inform the company of any changes in circumstances which are likely to affect acceptance of the risk or an increase in the premium, and some companies now point this out on renewal notices.

When the policy is received it should be read with great care, for two reasons: one is so that the insured can be in no doubt what is covered by insurance and what is not, and the second is to understand the general terms and conditions of the policy.

The main part of the policy will explain exactly what is covered and whether or not there is a sum of money – say the first £50 of any loss – to be borne by the insured, or if there is a limit on any sum payable. If a policyholder thinks such a sum in respect of any particular section of the policy is not enough for his requirements should a claim be necessary, the time to raise the matter, and negotiate increased limits with the concomitant increase in premium, is at once and not when the need arises.

Undoubtly the part of the policy which leads to more contention and, at times, accusations of sharp practice against insurance companies, is that section which outlines the general conditions. In many equine policies, the first clause is generally a condition that the insured warrants the animal in question, or any to be added to the policy during its life, to be in perfect health and free from injury and disease. This is wide ranging but, nevertheless, analogous to the principle of *uberrimae fidei* that is incumbent on the insured not to seek to deceive the insurance company by getting cover for an animal known to be in ill health, diseased or injured.

On the other hand, many animal owners complain that there are some equine diseases which may not be manifesting themselves at the time a policy is taken out, when the horse or pony in question appears to be fit and healthy. Only when a claim is made and the veterinary advisers to the insurance company, on examination, state that at the time the policy was taken out the animal must have been diseased, is there a refusal to meet the claim.

This is particularly tough on claimants, who argue with some justification, that the only certain way to know the true state of a horse's health is by a post-mortem examination. In this and similar cases much depends on the individual insurance company. Most, while voiding the claim, will return the premium while others might well seek to come to a without prejudice compromise and meet part of the claim.

Obviously what may be called standard policies will only cover run-of-the-mill situations. Injuries to horse and/or rider incurred during equestrian events, or point-to-point or other races, where there is a higher degree of risk will, in all probability, require more specialist policies of the type most likely to be underwritten at Lloyds. Here again, the need for utmost good faith is imperative, as is the need for the person seeking insurance to be crystal clear about his requirements. It is an exercise in futility *to seek to convince* those providing insurance cover that the insured really meant to cover against a particular eventuality – for which a claim is being made – rather than what was actually specified in the policy.

To avoid disputes as to what exactly is and is not covered by insurance, anybody seeking a specialist policy is well advised to spend time in thinking ahead for a year, which will be the duration of the policy, of risks likely to arise, what is required and the level of cover.

Once this has been done the person seeking insurance should consult a reputable insurance broker, giving him a written list of requirements and making it clear that the broker's professional skills are depended upon to effect the type of insurance cover required. The advantage of this method is that if the coverage provided is found to be inadequate, the rider has a claim in negligence against the broker for any subsequent loss. Needless to say, to establish such a claim it will be necessary to prove not only that the expertise of the broker was relied upon but that the broker was properly briefed as to the insurance requirements. Hence the importance of written instructions.

Most riders take sensible precautions and wear a hard hat when out riding. Many head injuries have had their potential severity reduced because the rider was suitably protected. If the accident was caused by a third party who was subsequently sued, lack of protective head covering could be a major factor in estimating damages for the injuries received. Almost certainly the person sued would claim that injuries would not have been so severe if protective head covering had been worn. If this can be medically proved, it is more than likely that a judge would rule that lack of elementary precautions on the part of the rider constituted contributory negligence and there would be a subsequent reduction in any damages awarded.

Appendix I: Where to sue and where

When the question of litigation arises, who to sue and in what court of law to initiate an action depend on the nature of the case.

If a horse owner has a dispute with a livery stable or a riding establishment, as a result of circumstances referred to earlier in this book, action will be taken either against the owner of the establishment or the company running it.

If litigation should follow as a result of an accident caused by another person, that is the person to sue. If the dispute concerns the sale of a horse or a claim for faulty tack or services carried out negligently, the other party to the transaction is the person to be sued.

Just as a minor – that is a young person under the age of eighteen – cannot enter into a legally binding contract except for necessities, any legal action he wished to enter into has to be brought by his 'next friend', usually his parent or guardian, who is liable for the payment of any costs which may be awarded if the minor loses the case. A minor who is sued defends the case through his guardian *ad litem*, again almost certainly a parent or guardian who is not responsible for any costs which may be awarded.

There are two types of damages which can be claimed: liquidated or special damages and general damages. If, as a result of injury or maltreatment by a veterinarian, a horse suffers, the major claim may well be under the head of special damages. These are also known as liquidated damages as they can be quantified precisely: for instance, veterinary fees, medicines, etc are easily added up, as is the cost of replacing any tack, clothing or anything else damaged or destroyed in an accident.

Similarly, out-of-pocket expenses and money lost through inability to work can be quantified. What cannot be quantified in the case of injury to a rider is the financial compensation to cover pain and suffering or the potential loss of enjoyment if, as a result of an accident, the person's ability to ride is severely curtailed or lost completely.

Future loss of earnings cannot be quantified easily, for a number of imponderable factors, as well as age, have to be taken into account: for instance chances of promotion or upward progress in a chosen career. In the case of a woman, these factors may be further complicated by whether or not she is likely to become a housewife and mother.

Damages awarded to cover these losses are known as general damages and quite often riders who suffer severe injury as a result of someone else's negligence may wait two or more years before receiving any recompense. Many blame either their own legal advisers or the system, if not both, for the delay which may occur. In many cases this is unfair: anyone who is so severely injured that his future prospects are in doubt, should never rush to accept a settlement. In many cases it can take a considerable length of time before the full extent and effect of an injury can be determined with any exactitude. Once an offer has been accepted the claim is considered settled and no further sums can be claimed, even if the injury and its incapacitating effects may be worth, in terms of monetary compensation, much more than the sum accepted. However, if liability is admitted and only the amount of damages recoverable is in dispute, there is the new concept of interim payment, which allows money by way of compensation to be paid to the victim in advance of the final settlement.

Before a civil action is taken in the courts it is necessary to choose the right forum and this will be determined by the amount of money involved and/or the type of action to be brought. In all probability most actions will be brought in one of the 290 county courts in England and Wales which hear cases involving contract or tort in which the monetary value is no more than £5,000. They also deal with dissolution of partnerships and recovery of land as well as landlord and tenant matters. Debt, of course, which forms a large part of the work of a county court, comes under the heading of contract and a negligence claim is a tort.

In Scotland, there is no monetary limit to an action which is brought to the Sheriff Court although actions for over £500 may be brought in the Court of Session, the equivalent to the High Court in England and Wales. The High Court deals with all civil matters not dealt with in the county court.

In county courts, which are presided over by legally qualified judges, claims for less than £500 are dealt with by the Registrar – a solicitor – and proceedings are conducted in an informal manner. Although either or both parties to an action are entitled to be represented by a barrister or solicitor, unless the case is of a complicated nature costs for legal representation will not be awarded. In many cases, such as a dispute with a shop over the merchantable quality or otherwise of goods, the Registrar will sit as an arbitrator and there is a right of appeal from his decision to the county court judge.

County courts serve a most useful purpose in dealing with civil disputes and claims without the long delays which are sometimes a feature of an action started in the High Court. Many of the parties to actions in county courts conduct their own cases. In fact county courts have a supply of booklets outlining how to bring or defend your own case in such a court.

In county courts cases are started by the plaintiff issuing a plaint which sets out the claim and a summons which sets down the date on which the defendant is to appear. In most cases the Registrar will hold a pre-trial review, the aim of which is to either settle there and then, or decide whether the case is suitable for arbitration or trial, the date for which may then be fixed at this hearing. Cases in the High Court are started by a writ and then follow a number of formal stages before a case is set down for trial.

Whether a case comes before a county court or a High Court judge, the procedure is the same, with the plaintiff's case being opened by his lawyer – in the county court either a solicitor or

APPENDIX

barrister and in the High Court a barrister – which is followed by evidence of the plaintiff and that of any witnesses. At the end of the plaintiff's case the same procedure is followed by the defence and when all evidence has been called, the lawyers for both sides summarise their case and argue any points of law involved before judgment is given. An appeal on a point or points of law is to the Court of Appeal from both the High Court and a county court.

A similar procedure obtains in Scotland. An appeal from a Sheriff court on a point of law is to the Sheriff principal and from him, if he certifies a point of law is involved, to the Inner House of the Court of Session. The Scottish equivalent of the High Court is the Outer House of the Court of Session with an appeal on a point or points of law to the Inner House.

Litigation can be expensive but no one should be deterred from asking their solicitor at the first consultation whether or not he or she qualifies for Legal Aid.

Appendix II: Point-to-point Regulations

For many owners and riders one of the greatest thrills and benefits of their sport is the competition provided, whether it be at a local gymkhana, a three-day event, running their animals in point-to-point races or, for the good and even not-so-good horse, in a flat race or hurdle race under rules. Nevertheless, entering any of these events creates a legal obligation, the main thrust of which is that the competitor will abide by the rules not only of the event, but also of the ruling body of the particular sport. Indeed, the mere fact of entering a horse for a particular event would indicate that the owner is prepared to accept the obligation of abiding by the rules and regulations; and many conditions of events give judges and stewards wide powers which are deemed to be accepted by competitors.

A ruling body of any sport is entitled to make its own rules which will be binding on its members, and even maybe on non-members who participate in the sport, provided that the rules are originally approved by all those forming the particular body and that the correct procedure is followed for making subsequent changes. While the rules of a body remain in force, and this applies not only to such august institutions as the Jockey Club and the British Horse Society but also to a local riding club, they have to be followed. Any action taken by the particular organisation has to be within those rules.

Such rules may permit the expulsion of members and, as far as the Jockey Club is concerned as the ruling body of the sport, the right to fine a trainer or jockey or to withdraw or suspend a licence to train or ride, either indefinitely or for a fixed period. The Jockey Club may also 'warn off' anyone who has offended against the Rules of Racing, always provided that the person at risk is given the opportunity to defend himself against any allegations – this being a cardinal principle of what is known in general terms as natural justice, that no one should be condemned unheard.

There are some people who not only have a horse of sufficient calibre to justify racing it but also expertise and facilities to train it. This type of person will almost certainly be what is termed a permit holder under the Rules of Racing. A permit is limited to a person training only horses to run in steeplechases, hurdle races or National Hunt flat races and these horses have to be the sole property – with very limited exceptions – of either the trainer, his or her spouse, parents, sons or daughters; in other words, to be within the family.

The only exception to the requirement for horses to be trained by someone who has either a licence or a permit is for those animals competing in hunters' steeplechases, the Royal Artillery Gold Cup and the Grand Military Gold Cup. The criterion in these cases is that the horse may be trained privately by the proprietor of the stable from which the horse was regularly and fairly hunted during the current season.

The Jockey Club bans any rider from riding under Rules unless he is at least sixteen years of age and has a licence or permit, and this applies to the amateur as well as professional jockey. There are two categories of permits for amateur riders. Category A permits the holder to ride in any flat race, steeplechase or hurdle race which is confined to amateur riders and in all National Hunt flat races. A Category B permit allows holders to ride in flat races which are confined to amateur riders, in all steeplechases and hurdle races except those confined to licensed jockeys, and all National Hunt flat races.

The Jockey Club also lays down regulations for point-to-points, and horses taking part are restricted to two categories:

Steeplechases which are confined to the hunt or hunts promoting the meeting and/or one adjoining hunt if the horses are the property of either the master(s), members, subscribers or farmers and have been hunted during the season in which the point-to-point is taking place with the hunt or hunts concerned.
In all other steeplechases if a Hunter's Certificate has been issued in respect of the horse upon the form issued by the Stewards of the Jockey Club and lodged at the Racing Calendar Office.

Riders in point-to-point races must be more than sixteen years
of age and hold a Rider's Qualification Certificate for the season
in which they wish to ride. The certificate, which is issued by
the Masters of Foxhounds Association, must be signed by the
secretary of a hunt and outline a rider's particular
qualifications. Riders must also pay the required fee for the
personal accident scheme for those racing in point-to-points.

Rule 51 of the Jockey Club regulation for point-to-point races
states:

(i)   In races confined to a Hunt or Hunts the qualifications for
      riders shall only extend to:
      (a) The Master(s), Members, Subscribers, Farmers or their
          respective spouses or children of the Hunt or Hunts
          concerned who hold riders' qualification certificates for
          the current season from those Hunts.
      (b) If so provided in the conditions of the race, Serving
          Members of Her Majesty's Forces.
(ii) In Open Races the qualification for riders shall only extend to
      Master(s), Members, Subscribers, or Farmers of a recognised
      Hunt, or their respective spouses or children.
(iii) In Farmers' Races the qualification for riders shall only extend
      to those persons qualified to enter, their spouses, sons or
      daughters and if so provided in the conditions of the race,
      serving Members of Her Majesty's Forces.
(iv) In all other races only those persons qualified to enter horses
      shall be eligible to ride.

Rule 52 states that no restriction as to the sex of riders shall
apply except where a race (other than one for a club or society)
for riders of one sex is included in any programme, when a race
with similar qualifications of entry for riders of the opposite sex
must also be advertised.

Rule 53 lays down a number of categories of persons who are
not eligible to ride in point-to-point races. The object of this
Rule is to restrict riders to those who have never ridden for
payment under a professional rider's licence granted by any
recognised turf authority. A person who held an apprentice
jockey's licence or a conditional jockey's licence for no more
than twelve months from the date of issue of the first licence

may ride. An exception is also made for a person who held for not more than twelve months a steeplechase and hurdle race jockey's licence issued prior to July 1978.

A person whose principal paid occupation is, or at any time during the last twelve months has been, to ride or groom for a licensed or permitted trainer will not be eligible. A similar restriction applies to a person whose principal paid occupation has been as a groom in a private livery or horse dealer's stable or as a hunt servant.

Riders in point-to-point races are entitled to be paid expenses in very limited circumstances which are set out in an appendix to the regulations for point-to-point races drawn up by the Jockey Club.

It is obligatory for riders to wear skull caps which must be secured by a chin-strap and the only approved pattern is the one which reaches the British Standard BS4472 and carries the British Standards 'Kite Mark'. It must also be in a serviceable condition and correctly fit the rider. Also in the interests of safety is the strong recommendation of the Stewards of the Jockey Club that no riders should wear spectacles, while for those who wish to ride with contact lenses, the Stewards recommend the wearing of soft or perma-type lenses. There is also a further recommendation that a metal disc with an inscription indicating that the wearer is using contact lenses should be worn at all times during riding engagements. Discs can be obtained from the Licensing Department of the Jockey Club for a fee, at the time of writing, of £1.15 including VAT.

The following are prohibited substances under both the Rules of Racing and the regulations for point-to-point races:

Drugs acting on the central nervous system.
Drugs acting on the automatic nervous system.
Drugs acting on the cardiovascular system.
Drugs affecting the gastro-intestinal function.
Antibiotics, synthetic anti-bacterial and anti-viral drugs.
Antihistamine.
Anti-malarials and anti-parasitic agents.

Anti-pyretics, analgesics and anti-inflammatory drugs.
Diuretics.
Muscle relaxants.
Sex hormones, anabolic steriods and corticosteroids.
Endocrine secretions and their synthetic counterparts.
Substances affecting blood coagulation.
Cytotoxic substances.

A horse which has run in a point-to-point race and as a result of a routine dope test has been found to have traces of a prohibited substance in its body, or a substance which cannot be traced to normal feeding and which by its nature could affect the racing performance of the horse, will be disqualified. At the same time, unless the Stewards are satisfied that all reasonable precautions have been taken to avoid a breach of the rules, the owner will be fined not less than £525. Anyone who administers, attempts to administer, or causes or allows such substances to be administered, may be declared a disqualified person. However, when and if such cases of doping arise, those accused of the offence will not be condemned out of hand by Stewards of the Jockey Club, to whom a matter of such gravity will be referred.

The only way in which a disgruntled owner who is fined and/or declared a disqualified person may appeal against a decision of the Stewards of the Jockey Club is to show that he was denied natural justice or that the Stewards were acting *ultra vires*. The rules for point-to-point racing – as with those for National Hunt and flat racing – are laid down by the Jockey Club as governing body and, as with the governing body of any other sport, are binding on those who take part in the sport in whatever fashion which, after all, is only right and proper.

The law is loath to intervene in the way in which a sport is administered and sanctions imposed, if the rules of natural justice are followed. Today there can be no governing body of any sport which is not aware of the need to follow the rules of natural justice when dealing with matters for which sanctions are applicable. Furthermore, a judge would almost certainly take the view that any owner or rider of a horse should realise that by taking part in a race they are subject to the rules laid down by those responsible for administering the sport.

Appendix III: The Prevention of Cruelty

There are a number of laws which might be bunched together under the banner of legislation passed to prevent cruelty or unnecessary suffering and to maintain the welfare of horses.

For the purposes of the Protection of Animals Act 1911 and the Abandonment of Animals Act 1960, a horse, ass or mule is classified as a domestic animal. Under the Acts it is a criminal offence for either an owner or a person in charge of a domestic animal to abandon it without reasonable cause or excuse, whether temporarily or permanently, in circumstances likely to cause it unnecessary suffering, and this would constitute an offence of cruelty. It is not difficult to see, therefore, that the owner of a horse which was turned out into a field in the depth of winter without protective clothing and supplementary feed, and left unattended for some time, may be said to have temporarily abandoned the animal and therefore be guilty of an offence.

In criminal law a finding of guilt can only be sustained if a jury or a magistrate(s) are satisfied beyond reasonable doubt of the guilt of the accused, and one of the ingredients of any criminal offence is what the law describes as *mens rea*, that is, a guilty mind. In the case of the horse left in a field in inclement weather, it would be necessary for the prosecution to prove that the person responsible for the animal intended to abandon it temporarily and without reasonable excuse. As far as the suffering to the animal is concerned, this would be an objective test as to whether such abandonment was likely to cause unnecessary suffering. To prove such an offence might be more difficult than it would appear to be: it would be necessary, for instance, to show that the accused had knowledge of the potential severity of weather conditions and the lack of proper sustenance from the field itself, and that no precautions were taken either by way of a blanket or extra feed for the animal.

The Protection of Animals Act creates a number of offences of cruelty to animals which include beating, kicking, ill-treating, over-riding, over-driving or over-loading. Although it is safe to assume that all but a very small minority of horse owners treat their animals with kindness and consideration, it is also possible through ignorance for a horse to suffer when being transported. The Act makes it an offence if any person 'shall convey or carry, or cause or procure, or, being the owner, permit to be conveyed or carried, any animal in such manner or position as to cause that animal unnecessary suffering'.

Under this Act, in addition to imposing a fine and/or a sentence of imprisonment, a court has the power to deprive of ownership of an animal anyone who is convicted of cruelty and has a previous conviction for cruelty or against whom there is evidence to show further cruelty might take place. The owner does not need to have been the person who was the instrument of cruelty, as the Act states that an owner shall be deemed to have permitted cruelty if he failed to exercise reasonable care and supervision in respect of protecting the animal.

As long ago as 1915 it was held that in the case of a person knowing that a horse was in poor condition when it was bought and failing to prevent it from being worked, there was *prima facie* evidence of cruelty. It can be seen that there is an onus imposed on the owner of a horse to make sure that if it is in the care of another person it is not subject to cruelty.

An earlier piece of legislation – the Cruelty to Animals Act 1876 – makes it an offence to conduct an experiment on a horse, ass or mule without an anaesthetic unless it is certified that the object of such an experiment will be frustrated by the administration of an anaesthetic.

The Docking and Nicking of Horses Act 1949, which defines docking as the deliberate removal of any bone or part of a bone from the tail of a horse, prohibits docking and nicking unless a member of the Royal College of Veterinary Surgeons certifies in writing that such an operation is necessary, in his opinion, for the health of the horse because of disease or injury to the tail.

There is also a prohibition against landing a docked horse from outside the United Kingdom unless permitted by HM Customs and Excise or licensed by the Minister of Agriculture. A customs officer will give permission only if and when he is satisfied that the docked horse will be exported from the country as soon as possible, while the Minister will not grant a licence unless he is satisfied that the horse is to be used for breeding purposes.

The Protection of Animals Act 1934 makes it an offence for any person to promote, cause or knowingly permit to take place any live public performance which involves throwing or casting with ropes or other appliances any unbroken horse. It is also an offence to ride or attempt to ride any horse which by the use of any appliance or treatment involving cruelty is, or has been, stimulated with the intention of making it buck during the performance. Interestingly enough this Act can be said, even though unwittingly, to be an early piece of consumer legislation, for if a horse used for this purpose is represented to spectators as being unbroken and untrained it is on the defendant to prove the opposite case. Obviously, a trained and broken horse may well be able to take part in such a performance without suffering from cruelty or risking injury.

There are regulations which govern the transportation of horses by road, rail and sea which are really outside the scope of this book. Nevertheless, as these regulations were drawn up to protect the health and welfare of animals during transit, all owners and those responsible for horses should check that their chosen form of transportation meets the requirements which are laid down in the Transit of Animals (Road and Rail) Order 1975, the Horses (Sea Transport) Order 1952, and the Transit of Animals (General) Order 1973 which covers horses being transported by air.

Appendix IV: Exporting horses

Horses and ponies are frequently exported from this country and just as there are regulations, which have already been discussed, concerning the import of these animals so, too, are there regulations which govern exports, the main aim of which is to ensure that animals travel in conditions which do not cause distress or discomfort. At the time of writing, the Farm Animal Welfare Council, which was established in 1979 to keep under review the welfare of farm animals, including horses, in – among other things – transit, advises on any legislative or other changes which may be necessary.

As far as existing regulations are concerned, it is not lawful to ship, or even attempt to ship, any horse, mule or ass in any aircraft or vessel to any port or aerodrome outside the United Kingdom, the Isle of Man and the Channel Islands, unless a Ministry of Agriculture appointed veterinary inspector has certified that the animal is capable of being transported and disembarked without cruelty. It must also be certified as capable of being worked, presumably at the receiving country, without suffering. Further conditions specify that an inspector has to be satisfied the animal is not more than eight years old and in the case of a heavy draught horse is worth not less than £715. If it is a mule, a vanner (thought to be a horse capable of pulling a vehicle such as a milk float) or a jennet – a small Spanish horse – it must be worth not less than £495, and if an ass, not less than £220. These values may be altered.

An inspector's certificate is not needed regarding the conditions for conveyancing and disembarking if it is intended to use the horse as a performing animal or if it is registered in the stud book of a breed society recognised by the Secretary of State for Agriculture and is intended to be used for breeding or exhibition purposes. The other exception is if the animal is a foal at foot accompanying a horse registered in a recognised stud book.

When an exporter has been granted a certificate it has to be given at the time of shipment to the captain of the aircraft or the ship's master who will be transporting the horse. If during the course of transportation the horse suffers serious injury so as to be incapable of being disembarked without cruelty, the master of the vessel must have it slaughtered at once.

These provisions, as well as those concerning examination and certification of a horse, do not apply to the shipment of a thoroughbred horse which is certified by either a steward or secretary of the Jockey Club to have arrived in this country not more than one month before the date of shipment for the purpose of competing in a race, or is being shipped to run in a race or to be used for breeding purposes. It is still necessary for the certificate of the Jockey Club to be delivered to the master of either ship or aircraft.

Exemption is also granted in the case of any horse over 14.2 hands shipped to any port or aerodrome which is either in the Irish Republic or is not in Europe, any foal travelling with its dam, if it is the dam which is being shipped. A similar exemption from examination and certification will be granted to any horse over the same height if the Secretary of State for Agriculture is satisfied it is intended for exhibition, breeding, racing, riding, polo or jumping. However, a permit is required, which must be applied for at least seven days before shipment, although this time may be reduced in circumstances of genuine emergency. The same conditions apply to a foal travelling with its dam.

It may seem that these regulations are a bureaucratic nightmare but again it must be stressed that they have been drafted for the welfare of the animal which is to be exported. Additional regulations apply to ponies which, for these purposes, mean any horse not more than 14.2 hands in height, with the exclusion of a foal travelling with its dam if the dam is over 14.2 hands.

A permit is needed to ship or attempt to ship a pony outside the United Kingdom, the Channel Islands and the Isle of Man unless the Secretary of State for Agriculture is satisfied the pony is intended for breeding, riding or exhibition and:

It is of no less a value than £300;

In the case of a pony not more than 122cms high, other than a Shetland pony not more than 107cms high, is of no less a value than £200, or

If the pony is of the Shetland breed it is of no less a value than £145.

Immediately before shipment the pony has to be inspected by a veterinary inspector and certified fit to travel and be disembarked without unnecessary suffering. No pony will be certified as being capable of travelling if it is a mare and in the opinion of the veterinary inspector is heavy in foal, showing fullness of udder or is too old to travel or, if it is a foal, in the opinion of the inspector, it is too young to travel.

An offence is also committed if a registered pony is exported unless the secretary of the particular breed society issues an export certificate to the effect that the animal is registered in its stud book. In this context, a registered pony is one appearing in the Arab Horse Society Stud Book, the British Palomino Spotted Horse and Pony Society Stud Book or in the stud book of any of the following native breed societies: Connemara, Dales, Dartmoor, Exmoor, Fell, Highland, New Forest, Shetland and Welsh.

There are a number of legislative provisions which apply to the export of horses and ponies, including the Animal Health Act 1981, the Export of Horses (Protection) Order 1969, the Export of Horses (Veterinary Examination) Order 1966, the Export of Horses (Excepted Cases) Order 1969, the Export of Horses and Ponies (Increase in Minimum Values) Order 1969 and the Export of Horses and Ponies (Increase in Minimum Values) Order 1978. The last named enables the Secretary of State for Agriculture to adjust the values of horses or ponies as and when he sees fit.

Not only should anyone exporting horses or ponies be aware of these orders, they should also be aware of any health or welfare requirements of those countries to which a horse or pony is being exported. If there are to be intermediate stops on the way in a third country, the regulations there might apply as well. Anyone exporting a horse and/or pony is strongly advised to contact the Ministry of Agriculture, Fisheries and Food if they are uncertain whether or not the animal needs to have a licence or permit.

Transporting horses and ponies by both sea and air is a highly complex business and the Ministry of Agriculture, together with its sister departments in Scotland and Wales, issues a useful booklet. This contains the Code of Practice for transporting horses and ponies, including the approved method of humanely destroying animals should such a drastic step become essential in the case of emergency.

Appendix V: Where to ride

In general terms it can be said that a person may ride on public roads and common land unless it is expressly forbidden. No one can ride a horse over land belonging to another without the owner's express permission and to do so constitutes the civil wrong of trespass – notices that trespassers will be prosecuted are frequently seen.

To successfully bring a civil action for trespass it is necessary to prove damage to land, but a landowner has the right to use reasonable force to eject trespassers who refuse to leave. Nevertheless, many landowners have no objection to riders crossing their land provided they do so in a responsible fashion, causing no damage to growing crops or disturbance to cattle and sheep, and shutting gates after them. Bridleways, over which the public have right of way either on foot or horseback, do cross private land.

Common land may have specified paths on which riding of horses may or may not be permitted and riders using land of this type should check what rights they have to be there. Indeed, much common land or land set aside for recreational purposes by local authorities will have by-laws regulating where horses may be ridden and may specify that they should be ridden at not more than a walking pace or canter.

Not only local authorities but such bodies as national parks and nature reserves, and places such as Wimbledon Common, and New Forest and Epping Forrest, have by-laws controlling the use of their land. One of the biggest landowners in the country is the Forestry Commission, which has a standard set of by-laws applicable wherever land owned by the commission is situated. Unless permission is given in writing, a horse may only be led or ridden in the New Forest, on public bridleways on commission land or on bridleways specified by the Forestry Commission. It must also be remembered that land in the ownership of bodies such as those mentioned above may well bar grazing of horses unless permission has been granted.

Whether riding out on the public highway or over private land for which permission is given either to an individual rider or generally by way of by-laws, a standard of reasonable behaviour should always be maintained, not only in respect of the land itself but also towards other users. Many legal problems concerning horses arise because of unreasonable behaviour either by the riders and/or owners or those with whom they come into contact.

The ownership of a horse, the thrill of riding a responsive animal, either for sheer pleasure or in competitive events, should not be spoilt by such problems. In that respect at least, owner and rider are masters of their own fate.

Acknowledgements

In writing a book of this type the author is always indebted to a large number of people who provide not only encouragement but also help and advice. Most important of the many people who fall into this category is Richard Gordon, barrister-at-law, who acted as consultant editor yet again for one of my books and who has been invaluable in many ways. If there are any mistakes in law they are mine and not his.

Thanks are also due to the Jockey Club for permission to use extracts from their rules covering Point-to-Point racing, and in particular Mr Peter Twite, the head of administration of that august body.

I received invaluable help from civil servants at the animal health and welfare departments of the Ministry of Agriculture at Tolworth, Surrey: to them, much thanks.

I must also acknowledge help received from the Royal College of Veterinary Surgeons and the Veterinary Defence Society as well as a number of insurance companies specialising in the field of equine insurance.

Finally, and most important, I am very much indebted to Miss Cathinka Wells who typed the final manuscript and to the editor and publisher of Your Horse for their permission to use the two agreements for buying a horse and leasing grazing land which appear in the book.

Index

156